This book is dedicated to all the men and women who worked so hard to ensure a quality education for the children of Isolate School Boards.

Special thanks to my wife Gale, Jana and Rob Roy and Dorothy Nicholls who each assisted with the writing, editing or formatting of this book.

BIG
Isn't Better!

The History of Northern School Resource
Alliance and Its Predecessor Co-operatives
in Northwestern Ontario

Fred Porter

BALBOA
PRESS
A DIVISION OF HAY HOUSE

Balboa Press books may be ordered through booksellers or by contacting:

Balboa Press
A Division of Hay House
1663 Liberty Drive
Bloomington, IN 47403
www.balboapress.com
1 (877) 407-4847

Because of the dynamic nature of the Internet, any web addresses or
links contained in this book may have changed since publication and
may no longer be valid. The views expressed in this work are solely those
of the author and do not necessarily reflect the views of the publisher,
and the publisher hereby disclaims any responsibility for them.

The author of this book does not dispense medical advice or prescribe the use
of any technique as a form of treatment for physical, emotional, or medical
problems without the advice of a physician, either directly or indirectly. The
intent of the author is only to offer information of a general nature to help
you in your quest for emotional and spiritual well-being. In the event you use
any of the information in this book for yourself, which is your constitutional
right, the author and the publisher assume no responsibility for your actions.

Any people depicted in stock imagery provided by Thinkstock are
models, and such images are being used for illustrative purposes only.
Certain stock imagery © Thinkstock.

Printed in the United States of America.

ISBN: 978-1-4525-9688-4 (sc)
ISBN: 978-1-4525-9689-1 (e)

Library of Congress Control Number: 2014907835

Balboa Press rev. date: 05/06/2014

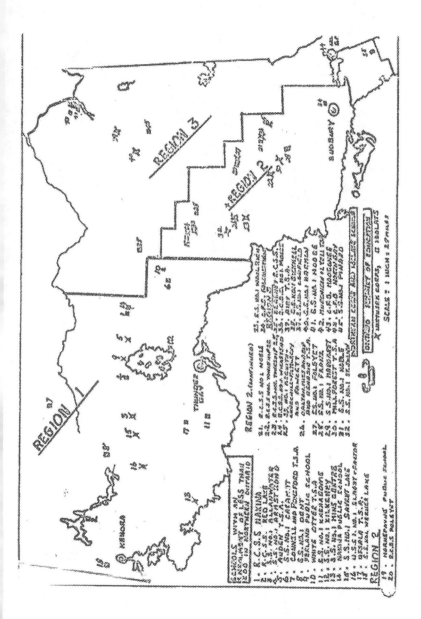

Contents

Introduction

This is the history of the Northern School Resource Alliance and its predecessor co-operatives in Northwestern Ontario. It is a story born out of a concern for the quality of education in rural and remote parts of the region. It is a story of a lack of resources at the Ministry of Education's Regional Office in Thunder Bay and a directive to reduce or eliminate direct services to isolate school boards (as defined in the General Legislative Grant Regulation [GLG] as having fewer than 300 pupils).

Born out of necessity was a co-operative effort of French, English and Aboriginal isolate school boards, both public and separate. What started as a small Co-operative Services Unit of the Umfreville District School Area Board [DSA] in 1977 grew into a non-profit Northwestern Ontario School Boards' Co-operative Services Program in 1990 and finally the Northern School Resource Alliance in 1997.

During the years from 1977 to 2010, the co-operatives provided both direct services to pupils (i.e. Territorial Students Program) and second level services to the school boards from professional development to financial services to classroom support for teachers.

While in its infancy, the Ministry funded those services and often the isolate boards had little say in how the service was delivered. Over time, this evolved into the isolate boards, renamed in 1996 as school authorities, choosing to be members or not of the Co-operative. Members paid an annual membership fee and were provided services at cost. Non-members paid no membership fee and were charged 20% over cost for services. A board of trustees selected by trustees of member boards governed the co-operative. The Ministry of Education funding model provided the school authorities with both funding and choice. The co-operative model provided the school authorities with choice, autonomy and support.

In June of 2009, without consultation, the Ministry of Education announced that the school authorities would be amalgamated with district school boards. When trustees of the school authorities threatened the Ministry with a judicial review, the Ministry passed a regulation freezing the assets of the Northern School Resource Alliance, placing them under the control of a district school board.

The co-operative model of education of school authorities that was in place from 1977 to 2009 came to an end on March 31, 2010. Today those school authorities of Northwestern Ontario are now administered by larger district school boards. Many of those schools have no governance representation on the district school boards.

What follows is the details of that 32 year journey.

[Note: Endnote exhibits are available for a nominal charge by contacting the author at fporter@tbaytel.net]

CHAPTER ONE

Isolate Boards and the Ministry of Education Regional Office in Northwestern Ontario in the Years 1966 to 1977

On April 1, 1966 Ontario Department of Education Superintendent A. H. McKague issued a memorandum announcing special assistance for small boards. In that memorandum,[1] he expressed concern about the qualifications and competence of teachers in small isolated schools. He proposed to recruit a volunteer corps of up to 16 young teachers with the energy and interest to go into isolated areas where adequate home accommodation could be provided.

In 1967, Canadian National Railway withdrew the school cars on the Northern CN line. This resulted in several villages along the main line of the CN without schooling for their children. Every seven miles there continued to exist tiny settlements inhabited by section crews, hunters, trappers and fishermen whose children still needed opportunities to have education without having to travel to a distant community to attend school. On the CN north line hamlets such as Ghost River, Allanwater Bridge, Collins and Ferland had been regular stops of the school cars. Since prompt action needed to be taken to respond to children's educational needs, the then Department of Education established small district school areas. Management was entrusted to three local trustees with a secretary-treasurer.

The Department of Education acted to build schools in hamlets on that railway line. In 1967 a one classroom school and teacherage was built at Allanwater Bridge. This was followed in 1968 with two classroom schools and teacherages in the hamlets of Auden and Ferland.

Also in 1967 the Ministry of Municipal Affairs handed over the administration of USS Number 1 Slaght and Factor (Umfreville District School Area Board) to the Regional Office of the Ministry of Education.

Many of the activities of the isolate school boards were overseen directly by personnel from the Regional Office of the Ministry of Education. It was recognized that there was educational and administrative challenges in dealing with isolate schools. In March 1970 Dr. R.R. Steele issued a memorandum to Dr. J. R. McCarthy, Deputy Minister of Education proposing "a manageable number of isolated schools be grouped with regard to (at least) some degree of geographic cohesion under the jurisdiction of an elected Board of Trustees".[2] The recommendation was not implemented.

In April of 1972, the staff of the Business Section of the Ministry of Education Regional Office looked at their operation and attempted to emphasize the urgency of a solution of the "Isolate Board" problem found in the region.[3]

In March of 1973, a study committee, consisting of area superintendents representing each of the three northern regions of the Ministry of Education, was formed to *review in depth the current status of Northern Corps schools and other isolated schools in the North*.

In July of 1973, the study committee filed its report "A Review in Dept of the Current Status of Northern Corps Schools and Other Isolated Schools in Northern Ontario."[4] The report dealt, in part, with the business support required for isolate boards. It was recommended that a local secretary should be retained by all isolate boards for day-to-day duties. It was further recommended that the use of contracted board auditors as accountants for the boards be discouraged. Also recommended, an assistant should be included on the Regional Business Administrator's staff to answer the needs of isolate boards and visit with board secretaries when required.

In November of 1973, Memorandum C, 1973-1974 was issued for the reorganization of "Regional Services of the Ministry of Education."[5] The memo clearly established a new role for the Ministry with the operation of school boards being viewed as the sole responsibility of the elected and/or appointed trustee(s). The memo indicated a coming reduction of Regional Office staff over the next few years and a "flat-line" restriction of the Ministry's budget.

As a result, the Regional Office attempted to involve each Board's auditor in the provision of improved financial and accounting assistance to school board secretaries, a function no longer the responsibility of the Ministry of Education.

In December of 1974 H. K. Fisher, Assistant Deputy of the Ministry of Education issued a policy memorandum outlining the relationship between public and separate school boards, isolates, those without a chief executive officer and school boards on crown lands.[6]

While shrinking resources and changing roles were placing increasing pressure on the Regional Office personnel, the education function in the isolate schools was continuing. Indeed, in some locations, new challenges were growing. People of Aboriginal origin were in some cases leaving their traditional communities and moving onto provincial crown land. Thus in 1976 the people of Slate Falls (75 air miles north of Sioux Lookout) and the people of Summer Beaver (200 air miles northwest of Geraldton) were granted permission to organize school boards.

The pressure on the Regional Office of the Ministry of Education continued to build while the needs of the isolate schools continued to increase. Clearly, a new model of support for these schools was urgently required.

Slate Falls School

Aerial view of flying into Summer Beaver

CHAPTER TWO

A New Service Model 1977

By the fall of 1976, the Regional Office of the Ministry of Education looked at two options to resolve the administrative pressures that the isolate school boards were placing upon Ministry resources in Northwestern Ontario.

On October 14, 1976 Superintendent of Business and Finance, Peter Workman sent a memo to Mr. J. Martin, Director of School Business and Finance[7] in which he outlined two options. Option one was to establish a separate unit for the isolate boards within the Regional Office which would mean Ministry personnel would serve the isolate boards in an administrative capacity. Option two was to initiate the formation of a co-operative staffed by board employees with services financed as part of each board's isolate board grants on a shared cost basis.

By November 1976 Dr. H. K. Fisher, Assistant Deputy Minister of Education, approved the second option in principle. The Umfreville Board was to govern a school services unit. An Isolate Boards Staffing Plan for Co-operative Management Services was drawn up.[8] This plan laid out the roles and responsibilities of the isolate board secretary, the supervisory services officer, the business administrator of the Co-operative and a clerk-bookkeeper.

Peter Workman (Photo taken in 2001)

From left to right Dennis Knight, Jill Zachary, Irene Nawagesic
(Photo taken in 1983 at Dennis Knight's 60th birthday)

A three-year plan was developed from the period of October 1976 to January 1978. In October of 1976, the isolate boards of Slate Falls DSA, Summer Beaver DSA and Sturgeon Lake DSA were to be serviced by the Co-operative. In January of 1977, the isolate boards of Allanwater DSA, Auden DSA, Ferland DSA and Umfreville DSA were to be added. Finally in January 1978, the isolate boards of Armstrong DSA, Caramat DSA, Kashabowie DSA, Kilkenny DSA, Mine Centre DSA, Savant Lake DSA, Upsala DSA and White Otter DSA were added. A Staffing Schedule and Proposed budget were developed.[9] It would begin at $8,300 in 1976 and grow to $50,000 in 1978.

An advertisement was prepared for an accountant and Mr. D. A. Knight was the first Business Administrator of the fledgling Co-operative.

On November 26, 1976 the Umfreville DSA Board met with Dr. R. Steele, Regional Director of the Northwestern Ontario Regional Office. Dr. Steele outlined the need for the Board to establish a school services unit to sell services to other boards that had been approved by the Assistant Deputy Minister. As a result, the following motion was passed: "The Umfreville DSA establish a School Services Unit effective January 1, 1977".[10] The Co-operative Services Unit of the Umfreville DSA Board was born. A new model of service delivery to isolate school boards was created.

On December 20th, 1976 Dr. R. R. Steele prepared a memorandum detailing his approval of the model.[11] Adjustments were made to the original three-year plan. Effective January 1, 1977 the Co-operative Services Unit was responsible for the entire business and accounting function for the following boards: Allanwater DSA, Auden DSA, Ferland DSA, Slate Falls DSA, Sturgeon Lake DSA, Summer Beaver DSA and Umfreville DSA.

Further, Dr. Steele indicated in his memo that it would be the policy of the Regional Office to encourage isolate boards to make use of the Co-operative's services on a voluntary basis.

The financing of this venture was to be financed by the Ministry under the isolate board provisions of the GLG Regulation. In turn, office and staffing costs were to be charged to each participating board using some appropriate base for cost sharing purposes.

Finally, the Regional Office supported a person to work with each board at the local level. That person would act as secretary to the board while the Co-operative Business Administrator would act as treasurer. A final operating budget for 1977 was established at $35,668.[12]

A memo to file was signed by Dr. Steele on March 23, 1977.[13] That memo summarized the model and made it clear that the Co-operative was a non-profit arm of the Board of Trustees of the Umfreville District School Area Board. That memo also made clear that the control of its costs would be exercised through the approval by the Ministry of the Umfreville Board's annual budget and the budget of each participating board.

Thus on January 1, 1977 the model was in place.

CHAPTER THREE

Growth of the Co-Operative Services Program

While the formation of the Co-operative Services Unit of the Umfreville DSA Board was largely driven by the demands for financial accounting and reporting, other challenges could also be identified.

By 1977, it was difficult to find people to act as school trustees. A major cause of that difficultly was the departure of families as woodland operations moved on and railways reduced jobs. This also resulted in declining enrolment in the schools.

Buildings were in need of extensive repairs and utilities/services such as generators, water systems and septic fields were beginning to experience breakdowns, suggesting a need for more frequent maintenance. Changes in railway schedules and policies were making some of the schools more difficult to service and supervise.

There was a disparity in the resources and support services available to children. Parents in some communities complained that they did not really possess any control over the education of the children.

Frances Poleschuk, Regional Director of the Northwestern Regional Office moved to make some changes to upgrade educational opportunities available to children.

Since residents of some small villages along the main line of the CN had expressed concern about absentee trustees, the DSA boards (Allanwater, Savant Lake, Armstrong, Ferland and Auden) were combined under a single large board named the

Northern DSA, with headquarters in Armstrong. The Northern DSA Board was also selected by the Ministry as a pilot project for the implementation of Bill 82 (Special Education). With the reorganization came a supervising principal, a special education consultant, a program supervisor and two itinerant special education teachers. It now meant that the children in these schools would have more resources and support.

The original services provided by the Co-operative Services Unit were also expanding from only financial services to include teacher support and maintenance. DSA boards shared the costs through their own budgets and determined which services that they required.

By 1981, the Co-operative Services Unit was made up the following personnel:

- A supervisory officer who was a Regional Office staff member responsible for overseeing all operations of the Co-operative Services Unit;
- A business administrator having the overall responsibility for directing the financial services to board as they requested;
- An accountant who worked under the direction of the Business Administrator;
- An education officer expert in native language (Ojibwa) instruction;
- An education officer to work with principals and trustees in professional development and to assume responsibility for the establishment of an educational resource unit;
- A specialist in special education; and
- A full-time maintenance person to service the boards

The Educational Resource Unit was established to provide teaching materials and other assistance to teachers in remote schools. Through the year, the Education Officer provided professional development on leadership for trustees and principals.

Another challenge was the issue of support for secondary students to continue their schooling in Thunder Bay. None of the DSA boards at that time provided secondary school education.

The Territorial Students Program was established to support those students in Thunder Bay from the isolate school boards. The counsellors were responsible for getting the students to and from the city as well as finding suitable board and lodging homes. They assisted students with personal problems both in and out of school. The counsellors were expected to maintain a liaison between the board home parent and the student's parent. They provided recreational opportunities for those students.

By 1981, the cost of operating the Co-operative Services Unit had grown to almost $300,000 annually.[14]

With the growth of the Co-operative Services Unit, changes were taking place at the community level. The need for teachers in the northern schools increased while a decrease of hiring was happening in the urban centres. Secondments, hiring and retention of teaching staff in northern schools occurred. New leadership was needed and obtained through the hiring of a Supervising Principal (Fred Porter) and Special Education Consultant (Grace Farrell) at the Northern DSA Board.

New schools were beginning to be built to replace aging structures. A new school in Connell and Ponsford DSA Board (Pickle Lake) was opened in the spring of 1981. A portable school was placed in Savant Lake to replace the aging building. A new school was built in Upsala. New teacherages were built in Armstrong, Allanwater Bridge, Savant Lake and Upsala providing housing for staff that was not otherwise available or adequate.

In 1984, the Regional Office of the Ministry of Education arranged for a Supervisory Officer to provide more time and leadership to the Co-operative Services Unit. Approximately 30% of the time of Larry Fontana, the Director of the Atikokan Board of Education was purchased and the title of Manager was assigned. This step meant the Co-operative Services Unit would have more proactive educational leadership available to its personnel.

Larry Fontana at the original Umfreville site

However, as the trustees and principals became more knowledgeable (both because of increased professional development and longer retention), concerns began to be voiced.

There were concerns about the perceived lack of financial and service accountability of the Co-operative Services Unit. By 1988 its budget has grown to $800,000.

There was concern by the Ministry of Education officials about the legality of Umfreville DSA with appointed trustees and no students. The school in Umfreville burned down in the late 1970's. Parents moved away leaving the board intact but with no students.

There was a question about the relationship among the Ministry, the Co-operative Services Unit and the isolate boards. Who made the decisions? Should the funding go the Co-operative Services Unit directly or to the participating boards?

With these growing concerns, The Regional Ministry Office arranged for an external review of the services provided by the Co-operative Services Unit of the Umfreville DSA Board. In 1998, Reg Jones, Superintendent of Business and Plant, Lakehead Board of Education, Mr. Len Yauk, Director of Education and Secretary, West Parry Sound Board of Education and Mr. Dave Marshall, Dean Faculty of Education, Nipissing University College (Laurentian University) carried out the review. The Ministry contact for the review team was Mr. Jim Whicher, Supervisory Officer for the Umfreville DSA Board.

REFLECTIONS ON THE NORTHERN
SCHOOL RESOURCE ALLIANCE

Luke Schill, Former Consultant
Umfreville DSA Board Co-operative Services Unit
Fort Frances, Ontario

Additional Memories That You Would Like to Share?
I recall a forced landing on Hicks Lake, a crash landing at Slate
Falls and having the pilot fall asleep when one tank ran out of
gas. I also remember you (Fred Porter) and I flying with Air
Ontario from Pickle Lake to Thunder Bay. We were flying in
freezing rain when we hit what I think was an air pocket. To
say the least it was a weird feeling as we went into free fall. Who
could forget about the machete episode!

REFLECTIONS ON THE NORTHERN SCHOOL RESOURCE ALLIANCE

Diane Laybourne, Chairperson
Northern District School Area Board
Armstrong, Ontario

What did the Co-operative mean to your local school?
The Co-op provided much needed guidance to the principals we had over the many years that I was involved in the school as a parent and school board member. We were chosen for various pilot projects mainly due to the Co-op's involvement. Our students benefited from many initiatives and projects that were managed through the Co-op.

What impact did the Co-operative have upon your community?
My involvement with the Co-op stared in the middle 1970's. The Co-op was the most important connection the community had regarding the Ministry. We were kept informed on the many changes made by the Ministry and were able to understand the reasons for those changes through the involvement from the Co-op.

Additional Memories That You Would Like to Share?
I met many interesting people and was always thankful for the help and guidance and management skills that Fred Porter and his staff provided to Armstrong Public School staff, students and parents.

CHAPTER FOUR

The Service Model Reviewed

The purpose of the review was to look at the provision of co-operative services to the seventeen isolate school boards in Northwestern Ontario by the Umfreville DSA Board.

The review team designed specific questions to provide a guide for their research activities. The questions were divided into two parts.

First, with regard to the isolate school boards of Northwestern Ontario: a) What needs (business/educational/student) now exist which cannot be efficiently met by the boards themselves; b) to what extent are these being effectively met by the Umfreville operation; c) To what extent are they not being effectively met by the Umfreville operation; d) What alternative approaches could be considered, and what are the financial, social and political implications of each; e) What relationships exist among the client boards, the Umfreville Co-operative Services Unit and the Ministry of Education? What relationships should exist?

Secondly, with regard to the Umfreville DSA Board: a) To what extent is the current method of funding the board operation effective or ineffective? Is there a better method? What is it and what are the implications of adopting it; b) To what extent is the current organizational model effective or ineffective? How can it be improved; c) To what extent does the present location in Thunder Bay enhance or inhibit the effectiveness of its operation? What other locations, if any, should be considered, and what are the implications of moving the operation to each?

The research was approached as a field study in which a sample of the isolate boards provided the context from which to obtain interpretive data. This data was supplemented with basic data about the Umfreville services provided by Umfreville DSA Board.

The study focused upon five service delivery areas: a) Professional Development Services; b) Consulting Services; c) Financial and Business Services; d) Territorial Student Program Services and e) Supervisory Officer Services.

Due to time and travel constraints, only a sample of the isolate boards was visited by the review team. The sample selected attempted to ensure as much as possible a fair representation of the isolates (rail access, road access, very isolated, close to a major centre, etc.) that were served by the Umfreville DSA Board. In addition, the sample selected must ensure representation from aboriginal constituents.

The isolate boards selected and personnel interviewed were as follows:

> **Mine Centre DSA**: Principal, Teacher, Board Secretary Treasurer, Board Chair
> **Atikokan Roman Catholic Separate School [RCSS] Board**: Principal, Board Chair
> **Upsala DSA**: Principal, two Teachers, Board Secretary Treasurer, Chair, Parents
> **Slate Falls DSA**: Principal, two Teachers, Secretary Treasurer, Chair, Parent
> **Connell & Ponsford DSA**: Principal, three Teachers, Secretary-Treasurer, Trustee
> **Nakina DSA**: Principal, two Teachers, Secretary-Treasurer, Chair, Parent
> **Armstrong DSA**: Principal, two Teachers, Secretary-Treasurer, Chair, two Parents, Supervising Principal.

The review team met individually with the five supervisory officers responsible for the isolate boards. In addition, Ministry information was provided by the Supervisory Officer for the Umfreville Board, Regional Superintendents of the Ministry of Education and the Regional Director of the Northwestern Regional Office.

Interviews were conducted with the Co-operative Services Unit consultants, the business administrator and staff as well as the Umfreville Manager and each trustee of the Umfreville DSA Board.

Following the collection and interpretation of the data, the review team released a report outlining 55 recommendations.[15] Central to the review and report was the organizational structure and funding of the Co-operative Services Unit as well its legality. The study showed that there was a strong consensus among the boards that the services of the co-operative services unit were necessary and appreciated. However, along with that, confusion was expressed by the boards as to whether the Co-operative Services Unit was their unit or simply an arm of the Ministry.

When the report was reviewed in the context of what later occurred, there were a number of recommendations, which became key to the organization over the next 20 years.

In the context of structure, key recommendations became the following:

a) That the Ministry of Education effect the appropriate legislation to create a Co-operative Services Unit for Northwestern Ontario Isolate Boards as an independent Schedule 1 agency of the province of Ontario.

b) That the Board of Directors of the Northwestern Ontario Isolate Board Co-operative Services Unit consist of five directors drawn from existing isolate boards trustees on a rotational and representational basis and replace the existing Umfreville Board.

c) That the Northwestern Isolate Co-operative Services Unit be provided with a full time Director of Education and Secretary to the Board for the equivalent.

d) That the Co-operative Services Unit Board meets at least quarterly and that it convene one annual general meeting with representation from each board.

e) That the Co-operative Services Unit develop by-laws and terms of reference for the new agency to be ratified at the first meeting of the newly formed agency.

f) That the Co-operative Services Unit be funded by the Ministry of Education as an agency of the province.

g) That the business services provided by the Co-operative Services Unit to each isolate school board be clearly defined and included in an individual three year agreement with each isolate board.

h) That supervisory services be provided by officers who have been contracted by the Co-operative Services Unit and not be provided by the Ministry of Education.

i) That the consultants, under the direction of the "Director" of the Northwestern Isolate Co-operative Services Unit and in consultation with the isolates and the Ministry, establish a) a common role description and b) an annual set of curriculum/program relative objectives for their services.

j) That a necessary component of the in-service sessions for trustees be an annual general meeting of the directors comprising the Co-operative Services Unit.

k) That a review and examination of the framework and functioning of the Territorial Student Program be undertaken.

The review of the services provided by the Co-operative Service Unit of the Umfreville DSA Board was made public. The concerns of the isolate boards were heard and summarized. The need for a co-operative model to support the isolate boards was reinforced. A number of recommendations would in whole or in part become key elements of the evolution of the cooperative model in Northwestern Ontario.

With that in mind, the Regional Director of Education held a management retreat of the Regional Office. The report was reviewed and key decisions made to allow for the next phase of the co-operatives resolution.

In September of 1988 the management team of the Northwestern Ontario Regional Office submitted to Roy Houghton, Assistant Deputy Minister, Learning Services Divison "A Proposal for the Restructuring of the Umfreville DSA Board and the Co-operative Services Unit Which It Administers". The proposal provided recommendations for short and long term restructuring of the Board and its Co-operative Services Unit.

The proposal was supported by Assistant Deputy Minister R. Houghton and in turn submitted to Dr. B. Shapiro, then Deputy Minister. Approval was given for the short term restructuring of the Umfreville DSA Board for a two-year pilot basis. Implementation of the pilot project would commence on January 1, 1989 with the understanding that it would be reviewed by December 31, 1990.

REFLECTIONS ON THE NORTHERN
SCHOOL RESOURCE ALLIANCE

Bert Johnson, Chairperson
Upsala District School Area Board
Upsala, Ontario

What did the Co-operative mean to your local school?
The Co-operative meant everything to our school in Upsala. To our teachers, it offered professional development and support in any problem that might arise. To our administration, it also offered professional development, accounting and administration aid as needed. Trustees and board staff were encouraged to tap into the human resources of the Co-op. The Upsala DSA Board was able to maintain its autonomy and independence as a small, unique school and board through the support and guidance of the Co-op.

What impact did the Co-operative have upon your community?
Because of the Co-operative we were able to keep our school operating as an independent entity. Without the Co-operative co-ordinating all of the services that all of the isolate school boards in our region needed, all our communities would not have been able to keep our schools open on our own.

Through working together we were able to keep our independence.

Additional Memories That You Would Like to Share?
The Co-operative was a lifeline to the school in our community. All of the staff at the Co-op were very helpful and professional.

The Co-op allowed the schools in our communities to thrive and to offer a quality education to the children in our care.

CHAPTER FIVE

The Pilot Project 1988-1990

The restructuring proposal, approved by the Deputy Minister for implementation beginning January 1, 1989, called for both a short term and long term restructuring.

The short term restructuring was approved as a two-year pilot project. It provided for the following:

1. That the contract of Larry Fontana (part time Manager of the Umfreville DSA Board) be terminated effective December 31, 1988.
2. That Jim Whicher (Education Officer) be seconded on a full-time basis from the Regional Office to the Umfreville DSA Board for a two-year term to manage all the operations of the Board.
3. That a list of available, willing and competent supervisory officers be developed from which boards would be given the opportunity to choose, and that additional funding be provided to the Umfreville DSA Board in an amount equivalent to the cost of hiring two full time supervisory officers.
4. That Mike Vasco (Education Officer) be seconded from the Regional Office for a one year term to carry out responsibilities related to capital proposals and plans, plant operations and maintenance.
5. That the office of the Umfreville DSA Board be moved to a larger facility so as to provide sufficient working space for this increased staff.

The approval of the pilot project with these components proceeded with the understanding that any long term restructuring would occur as an outcome of the pilot project. Hence the Umfreville DSA Board passed the following resolutions on November 7, 1988:

1. That the Umfreville DSA Board, effective January 1, 1989 second a person to be Chief Executive Officer to the Board and Chief Administrative Officer of the Co-operative Services Unit and that this secondment be for a duration of two years commencing January 1, 1989 and ending December 31, 1990.

2. That the Umfreville DSA Board, effective January 1, 1989 second a person to be Capital and Plant Consultant for the Co-operative Services Unit of the Umfreville DSA Board and that this secondment be for a duration of one year commencing April 1, 1989 and ending March 31, 1990.

With those pieces in place, an amendment to Section 252 of the Education Act was included in Bill 69, which allowed two, or more isolate board to appoint a supervisory officer as director of education and facilitate further appointments of supervisory officers.

A cadre of supervisory officers were recruited to provide supervisory services to client boards. Boards were given the opportunity to select from this list or enter into agreements with other boards. A draft letter of agreement was prepared for the supervisory officer to sign outlining duties, expectations and reimbursement.[16]

Provision was made for the Umfreville DSA operation to move from 1820 Victoria Avenue in Thunder Bay to the old Green Acres School at 405 Isabella Street West in Thunder Bay.

This relocation, costing close to $450,000 allowed for additional space and modernization of systems.

To address the issue of isolate board ownership of Umfreville, an Umfreville Advisory Committee was created. The Committee was comprised of one trustee from each isolate board. Its mandate was to help guide the pilot projects implementation. Between February of 1989 and June of 1990 the Committee met six times. Much of its work was to make suggestions about the long-term organizational model and services levels.[17]

Official opening of Umfreville Co-operative Services Green Acres School site. From left to right Jim Whicher, Director of Education, Art Gouriluk, Chairperson of the Umfreville DSA Board, Fred Porter, Associate Regional Director of Education.

On June 30, 1989 Northwestern Regional Director of Education, Margaret Twomey issued an update on direct supervisory services to isolate boards.[18] Key pieces of that update included the announcement that actual implementation of the pilot project would begin on August 1, 1989. The memo also noted that Jim Whicher held the appropriate qualifications to be appointed director.

Business services were broadened. For smaller boards, the services included the processing of invoices and issuing of cheques, calculation of payroll and benefit administration, bank reconciliations, tax bill preparation and collection, preparation of audit working papers, budget preparation and other financial reporting. Larger boards would use fewer of those services.

By the summer of 1990, it was time to take a look at the pilot project, prepare a report and make recommendations. Fred Porter, Associate Regional Director of Education, undertook that process. On July 31, 1990 The Umfreville DSA Pilot Project Report was completed. The report was prepared at the request of Roy Houghton, Assistant Deputy Minister and was intended to provide information, examine the effectiveness of the pilot project and to provide recommendations regarding the long term restructuring of the Umfreville DSA. The report contained 21 recommendations.[19]

However, prior to the writing of the report, a key meeting was held on June 5, 1990. The meeting involved trustees and staff of the Umfreville DSA Board, the Umfreville Advisory Committee and Ministry personnel.[20] At this meeting, the services of the Co-operative Services Unit were discussed. The Advisory Committee expressed satisfaction with most services. In addition, there was discussion entered around the following: a) a two-tier board; b) governance and voting; c) membership and d) empowerment. The idea of a two-tier board to replace the present Umfreville DSA was supported by all including an agreement that the new board should be comprised of one trustee from each client board.

One of the key recommendations in the report was based upon the discussion from the June 5, 1990 meeting: *"That the Ministry of Education take the necessary steps (upon receipt of a formal request from Umfreville) to provide the legislation required to establish the two-tier model outlined in this report".*

The basis was established for a change to the existing cooperative model. However that would prove to take four more years to come to fruition.

REFLECTIONS ON THE NORTHERN SCHOOL RESOURCE ALLIANCE

Terry Swanson, Chairperson
Nakina District School Area Board
Nakina, Ontario

What did the Co-operative mean to your local school?
It meant a lot. The CEO and consultants spent a lot of extra time with staff, both in the school and office. Also some students gained from the information passed to the staff.

What impact did the Co-operative have upon your community?
It made our school system much richer for the knowledge imparted to them and benefited by this.

Additional Memories That You Would Like to Share?
I personally miss the dedication that was given by teachers, aides, other staff and also to members of the board.

CHAPTER SIX

Transition to a New Model

1990 began as a year of optimism for the Umfreville DSA Board and the Umfreville Advisory Committee. On October 12, 1990 the Board and Committee met with Fred Porter (then Director of Education of the Fort Frances Rainy River Board of Education) to discuss some of the recommendations made in the report on the Umfreville Pilot Project. As a result, the following motion was passed by the Umfreville Advisory Committee: *"That the Umfreville Advisory Committee supports acceptance of the report by the Umfreville District School Board"*.[21] That meeting and resolution clearly demonstrated the growing influence of the isolate boards upon the governance of the Umfreville Board.

Also noteworthy was the discussion around the potential names for the new board. One was The Northwestern Regional School Board and the other that most trustees favoured was the The Northwestern Co-operative Services School Board. Finally the Advisory Committee passed resolutions recommending the Umfreville DSA Board request a legislation be passed to create a two-tier school board and that the pilot project be extended until the new board began operation.

In response to the Umfreville DSA Board and the Advisory Committee, there were two significant pieces of communication. On November 30, 1990 Minister of Education Marion Boyd informed Terry Swanson, Chair of the Advisory Committee the following: *"You will be pleased to know that the Ministry's Management Committee has accepted a recommendation from the Northwestern Ontario Regional Office and has extended the pilot project for the Umfreville District School Area Board until August 31, 1991, so that services may continue to be provided to the isolate boards until the end of the 1990-91 school year".*[22]

On March 25, 1991 Regional Director of Education Jackie Dojack advised Umfreville Director Jim Whicher that she had requested the Management Committee of the Ministry to extend the pilot project for two additional years (from September 1, 1991 to August 31, 1993). In that correspondence Ms. Dojack identifies seven key questions/concerns that must be resolved before the Ministry would take further action.[23] Among those concerns listed was the need to await a report from the newly created Northern Project Unit of the Ministry of Education and legal issue of creating a board that has no resident pupils or schools.

The Northern Project Unit was established by the Ministry of Education with a mandate to determine cost-effective and efficient ways of improving education services to small and isolate boards in Northern Ontario. The release of the report was to occur sometime in 1992.

With that in mind, the Umfreville Advisory Committee responded to the concerns identified by the Regional Director Jackie Dojack. In that response, the first hint of frustration with the Ministry from the Umfreville Advisory Committee began to appear. The Committee responded as follows: *"We fully expect, on the basis of many precedents, that the Ministry will not implement the recommendations of the Northern Project without first referring them to an internal committee established to examine the impact We anticipate, therefore, a delay in implementation, not of two years, but of three, four or five years. By that time, conditions may have changed; the whole process may well have to begin again."*[24]

In response, on April 29 1991, Regional Director Jackie Dojack acknowledged that the process of developing and passing legislation is slow under the best of circumstances. She then advised that she had requested and received approval for a two-year extension of the pilot project.[25] It was the Ministry's intent that this two-year extension would allow for a variety of service arrangements to be tested with potential clients, subject to Regional Office approval.

During the next year, services continued to be provided to the isolate boards by the Umfreville DSA Board. However no resolution to Ministry delays were apparent. On December 6, 1992, the Umfreville Advisory Committee passed the following resolution:

"That whereas: The Umfreville Pilot Project has been operating successfully for close to three years; And whereas: Numerous communications, written and oral, for the purpose of solving problems and responding to questions, have taken place between this Advisory Committee and The Ministry of Education; And whereas: All concerns raised by the Ministry have been addressed by this committee; And where: The Ministry has now struck a new committee for the apparent purpose of re-examining questions which have already been answered; Be it therefore resolved: That the Umfreville Advisory Committee expresses its deep concern over what appears to be an unnecessary procrastination by the Ministry vis-à-vis the preparation and passage of requested legislation"[26]

In early 1993 the Northern Project Unit issued its findings. One key finding was the need for cooperation among school boards and other agencies. It noted that *"Boards support co-operatives provided that they spring from the grass roots, have voluntary entry and choice of services, protect the autonomy of participating boards and respect denominational and language rights"*.[27]

Then in the spring of 1993, conflict emerged between the two organizations. In a joint letter dated May 28, 1993 Regional Director Jackie Dojack and the Director of Umfreville DSA Board Jim Whicher signed a joint letter indicating an extension of the pilot project had been requested to August 31, 1996 or when legislation enabling the establishment of educational cooperatives was passed.[28] In that same letter there was also reference to reductions in funding and the reduction of the position of the Umfreville DSA Board Director to half time. The Umfreville DSA Board expressed their concern and the Ministry once again responded.

On August 26, 1993 Regional Director Jackie Dojack advised that the pilot project would be continued until August 31, 1994 and position of Director be full time for the period of September 1, 1993 to August 31, 1994. She also indicated that the Regional Office would work with isolate boards in the region to *"ensure a smooth transition from the current arrangements for services with the Umfreville DSA Board to alternate arrangements".*[29]

On a teleconference, September 28, 1993, the chairs of the isolate boards convened with the Regional Director present as well. The teleconference clearly represented a shift from the requested legislation to a co-operative model similar to the Ontario School Boards Insurance Exchange [OSBIE]. On that teleconference it was clear that the pilot project called Umfreville needed to come to an end.[30] It was also made clear that the onus for coming up with a new model other than a school board would rest with The Advisory Committee and the Board itself.

The concept of a joint venture, similar to OSBIE was born. Following that, research was done on OSBIE and legal advice sought. Consultation continued with the stakeholder and from that emerged the name of a joint venture: **The Northwestern Ontario School Boards' Co-operative Services Program**. An *"Agreement for School Boards, School Authorities, Education Authorities and Private Schools"* was drawn up. A governance structure was established and recruitment of a CEO was conducted.

The governance structure established called for a Board of Directors (each member was to appoint one trustee to sit on that board). From that group, an Executive Committee was to be elected. That Committee would include the Chairperson, Vice-Chairperson and three other members of the Board of Directors. The Board would be responsible for strategic matters while the Executive would act as a working committee and make recommendations to the Board. An organizational chart was established to guide the working of The Co-operative.[31]

Funding mechanisms were established. All income would be received from clients with no direct funding from the Ministry. The administrative costs of The Co-operative (estimated at $234,000 annually) were to be divided among members. Calculations were established for the division of membership fees as well as service costs.[32]

On May 6, 1994 the first meeting of the Board of Directors of The Northwestern Ontario School Boards' Co-operative Services Program was held.[33]

At that meeting, Terry Swanson (Nakina DSA Board) was elected the first chairperson of the new co-operative and Bert Johnson (Upsala DSA Board) the first vice chairperson. The rest of the Executive Committee was comprised of Ann-Marie Wesolowski (Red Lake Combined RCSS Board), Ed Morrissette (Atikokan RCSS Board) and Charlie Oskineegish (Summer Beaver DSA Board). By-Laws were approved and Fred Porter was appointed Chief Executive Officer and Attorney-in-fact effective September 1, 1994. Jim Whicher, Director of Education, was appointed Temporary Attorney-in-fact for the period May 6, 1994 to August 31, 1994. Michael Del Nin was appointed Business Administrator and Treasurer. Banking resolutions were passed.

Terry Swanson (Photo taken in 2001)

Finally the Board asked Director of Education Jim Whicher to write Regional Director of Education Jackie Dojack and express thanks for all their encouragement and assistance over the months and years that led to The Co-operative's formation. The frustrations of the past were replaced with delights at "<u>what we (all) have wrought together</u>".[34]

After several years of hard work and some frustration, a new model of co-operation was born.

REFLECTIONS ON THE NORTHERN
SCHOOL RESOURCE ALLIANCE

George Seaton, Chairperson
Connell and Ponsford District School Area Board
Pickle Lake, Ontario

What did the Co-operative mean to your local school?

It meant that we were not a small remote school standing alone-
but as a school belonged to an association of small schools-
with similar problems and difficulties that worked together to
provide the best possible education and support to our students.
(i.e. provided many programs such as literacy, tech support and
other locally identified needs). Provided work sessions that gave
opportunity to our trustees, principals, teachers, education
assistants and support staff to meet, discuss and work through
the common concerns of our students' needs throughout our
small communities.

What impact did the Co-operative have upon your community?

In general I feel the community was aware of the role the Co-
operative/Alliance played in support of our school and their
children-and that this organization supported their local
trustees and worked for the good of the children. It provided
much needed support and contact-when their children went out
for high school they knew they would be assisted in all aspects
of their children's lives-such as boarding home checks, school
attendance reports, extra-curricular activities, etc. ensuring
their children's lives were enriched by being part of this larger
educational experience.

Additional Memories That You Would Like to Share?

As a trustee on a small isolated board-one felt a real contribution was being made to all aspects of our students' education and not rubber stamping administrative decisions that our counterparts on larger boards appeared to do. Miss the camaraderie and friendships that were formed over the years.

CHAPTER SEVEN

The Cooperative Grows and Matures

There was much to do when September 1, 1994 dawned. The Co-operative Services Unit of the Umfreville DSA Board had been government funded. With that had been born a culture of dependency for the Co-operative Services Unit staff. The new model was self-funded by members and participants. Indeed, it now needed to operate as a business.

There were benefit programs, contracts and a collective agreement to be put into place, as well as a strategic plan, an increase in the client base and a positive cash flow needed. Development of a brand for the organization and marketing materials were required. Finally, and most importantly, there was the continuing need to provide quality services to the members and new clients in response to new Ministry initiatives.

Much of this was identified in the CEO Fred Porter's performance objectives dated November 18, 1994.[35] Over the next year, a collective agreement was reached with The Canadian Union of Public Employees [CUPE], which represented the unionized staff. As an attempt to re-culture the organization (to help staff understand that it was now operating as a business), a productivity bonus was introduced. The Ontario Municipal Employees Retirement System [OMERS] pension plan was transferred to The Co-operative for staff who were not part of the Teachers' Pension Plan. A similar request was made to the Teachers' Pension Plan which took several years for the status to be clarified.

A mission statement was developed. By the end of 1994, six new non-member participants had been added. That statement read as follows: "*The Northwestern Ontario School Boards' Co-operative Services Program is in business to provide customized administrative and curriculum services to members and clients in order to meet the educational needs in cost efficient* manner".[36] A fact sheet was developed to aid in marketing.[37]

Discussions were held with the Ministry to ensure that the isolate boards continue to have adequate funding. In December 1994 the isolate funding guidelines of the Ministry of Education's Northwestern Ontario Regional Office were released.[38] In those guidelines, the Ministry stated that for the September to December period (1994), boards would have access to funding for the services previously provided by the Umfreville DSA Board, Co-operative Services Unit. However the Ministry, in those same guidelines, made it clear that the boards could purchase services from different sources to provide the services for themselves. The boards would need to provide a plan indicating how they would maintain those services. It was clear that The Co-operative was operating in a new dynamic.

The Co-operative undertook other new initiatives. Internally, there was introduced the tracking of direct and indirect time allocations for billing purposes. A regular staff performance review process was introduced. Education consultants were required to negotiate performance objectives with client board staff. A linkage was established with board supervisory officers to ensure two-way communication and to address concerns in both directions. Externally, boards were given the opportunity to pool grants received for Family Violence Prevention and to collectively participate in order to get a "bigger bang for the buck". New policy support initiatives, including Safe Schools and Antiracism Ethno Cultural Equity were introduced for the boards who decided to participate.

Support initiatives for employment equity and transition years implementation were developed.

An auditor was retained and The Co-operative's financial activity was reviewed. The auditors' report, dated September 25, 1995 showed for the period September 1, 1994 to December 31, 1994 that The Co-operative has a $23,796 surplus as well as having placed $15,483 into a reserve fund.[39] Clearly, The Co-operative was off to a good start, in both services and financial perspectives.

1995 marked the first complete year of operation for The Co-operative. There continued to be 13 members, an application from a fourteenth board and the enrolment of 10 non-member participants.[40] Of particular note was the four boards from the Moosonee area, the first clients outside of Northwestern Ontario.

A number of short-term projects such as Violence Free Schools, Prevention of Violence Against Women and Preventative Maintenance Planning were completed. Project partnerships were formed with the Lakehead Purchasing Consortia and the Northern DSA Board. An external review of the Territorial Student Program was conducted by Ontario Institute for Studies in Education field office personnel resulting in support for services provided. The Co-operative Services Endowment Fund Organization was established providing bursary and scholarship awards for students of member boards.

While all of this was occurring, Ontario established a Task Force on School Board Reduction. Fred Porter, CEO and Mike Del Nin, Business Administrator made a presentation in Toronto to members of the Task Force. A strong case was made to maintain the existing isolate school boards and their co-operative.

In addition, a generic brief was prepared on behalf of the member boards. It was up to the member boards to customize that brief and submit it to the Task Force on School Board Reductions.

Finally, the transition from Umfreville DSA Board to The Co-operative continued. Information was provided to the Ministry of Education and Training regarding the value of Umfreville DSA Board assets and liabilities in order to have the Umfreville DSA Board statements finalized.

1996 marked the second completed year of operation for The Co-operative. By years end, membership had expanded to 17 member organizations. The non-member base also expanded.[41] The Co-operative's CEO would continue to advance the concept of expanding capacity without adding overhead.

An infrastructure partnership with the Consortium du Nord Ouest ensured both organizations would deliver services while minimizing overhead costs. The Co-operative's CEO also entered into discussions with the Ontario Institute for Studies in Education [OISE]/University of Toronto Northwestern Field Centre person, Wayne Seller, to explore programming partnerships.

1996 also saw The Co-operative's focus on First Nation issues. Slate Falls DSA Board services were began to be transitioned to the Slate Falls Education Authority. This was due to the creation of the Slate Falls Reserve by the federal government. The Program assisted the Education Authority with the transition by providing on site financial training.

The Co-operative also signed a contract with the Fort Frances Chiefs to provide research and support to their self-education governance initiative. Personnel such as Guy O'Brien, Jim Whicher and Florence Luke were retained to provide their expertise to that project.

In December of 1996 the Ministry of Education summoned representatives of all boards in Ontario to a number of sequestered meetings across the Province. At those meetings, the future of school boards in Ontario would be revealed.

REFLECTIONS ON THE NORTHERN
SCHOOL RESOURCE ALLIANCE

Armand Giguere, Chairperson
Caramat DSA Board
Caramat, Ontario

What did the Co-operative mean to your local school?
Support, peace of mind knowing that our children would receive the services they need to help them achieve their goals and fill their needs.

What impact did the Co-operative have upon your community?
Other than the trustees and school staff, I do not think that the community knew about the services that the Co-op provided.

Additional Memories That You Would Like to Share?
The memories would be knowing that our children got the best service and seeing so many people work well together-exactly what a Co-op is all about!! There could possibly be a lesson to be learned.

CHAPTER EIGHT

A Dodged Bullet 1996

During the past two years, the Province had examined the number of school boards in Ontario with a view to reducing numbers and saving money.

In December 1996, in a sequestered hotel room at the Airlane in Thunder Bay, the changes in what was titled *"Bill 104: Fewer School Boards Act"* were unveiled. The legislation, which would be passed in the Legislature in April of 1997, reduced the number of school boards from 128 boards of education to 72. The number of school trustees was reduced from 2,400 to approximately 700 with the November election of the new school boards. School board access to the property tax base was eliminated with the province to provide direct per pupil funding to the boards. The province also established the Education Improvement Commission to oversee school board operations and the restructuring process. The legislation provided for the existence of school councils.

The most interesting part of the restructuring was perhaps what did not happen. The 44 isolate school boards were given the name of school authorities and left untouched. Thus the isolate school boards would be known as school authorities but would continue to operate with the existing governance structure. The Co-operative would remain intact and continue to support the newly named school authorities.

The Co-operative and its clients dodged the amalgamation bullet. It would later be determined, as a result of a Freedom of Information request to the Ontario Ministry of Education, that the school authorities were left untouched as they represented an alternative governance model.

It is also interesting to note that in August of 1997, the Education Improvement Commission [EIC] issued a report called "*The Road Ahead*". In that report, the EIC note that the new district school boards "*will be able to save money using co-operative approaches among co-terminus and neighbouring school boards and multi-board consortia*".[42] The EIC in fact recommended, "*That co-operative services among co-terminus and neighbouring school boards and multi-board consortia be required, wherever possible and appropriate.*"

The recommendation mirrored the action taken by then isolate school boards and the Ministry Regional Office in Northwestern Ontario two decades earlier.

That dodged bullet, however, served to make the personnel of school authorities and The Co-operative much more vigilant about the actions that the Ontario Ministry of Education might take toward their autonomy and independence. As a result, The Co-operative began to take on a larger role of advocacy and political lobbying of the government in addition to the provision of quality service to the client organizations.

CHAPTER NINE

The Sigmoid Curve and the Northern School Resource Alliance

The Sigmoid Curve is an expression of success over time. That success can be measured in terms of profit, power or influence. In the context of a person, someone in the early stages of a career usually has negative productivity and effectiveness. There is an early loss to the company (salary without revenue) and to the person (education, clothes, relocation).

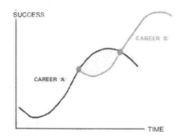

The Sigmoid Curve (http://vannevar.blogspot.ca)

Over time, that person figures out how to succeed and then success increases dramatically. During the growth period, success happens at an increasing rate, but in the maturity phase success occurs at a lesser rate. As the person ages, the sigmoid curve of this career ends in decline.

However there is an alternative for the person instead of decline. The strategy is to jump off the about to decline curve and begin a new curve. The new curve could be a complete make over of one's current job or a new job.[43]

If one applies that concept to an organization, it too can make the sigmoid jump. Organizations can make that jump by redefining their products or industry.

That concept can be applied to the new initiatives of The Co-operative, which began in 1997. In that year, The Co-operative, in conjunction with the member school authorities secured a $440,000 Technology Incentive Partnership grant (Project Isolate Northwest). This began the introduction of Internet and email technology to the school authorities.

The Co-operative also engaged in a strategic planning exercise, which saw an expansion of services available to member boards. The Co-operative also offered professional services (i.e. occupational health and safety, dispute resolution, human resources, purchasing, legal, architectural) at reduced rates using a brokerage model.[44] On May 30th of 1997 the passed a resolution approving the document Strategic Directions (1997-2000).

The long-standing issue with access to the Teachers' Pension Plan was resolved. The Co-operative arranged for the current CEO, Fred Porter, to be employed by the Nakina DSA Board as Supervisory Officer and then seconded back to The Co-operative for a portion of the time to carry out the duties of CEO. On November 28, 1997 the Ministry advised that *"approval of the matter was not one in which the Minister's approval is required"*.[45] This opened up the opportunity to employ recently retired teachers by The Co-operative to serve member clients.

On December 4, 1997 the Board of Directors passed a resolution amending the Bylaws and Letter of Agreement regarding membership in The Co-operative. The amendment addressed the issue of geography and specifically broadened the area of jurisdiction from Northwestern Ontario to Northern Ontario. Thus The Co-operative could begin to solicit clients and members from any part of Ontario north of the French River.[46]

1998 saw The Co-operative take on the role of co-ordinating the Regional Co-operative for Teacher Professional Development. The funding for the Regional Co-operative came from a grant from the Ontario Ministry of Education. A policy was put into place for the subsidy of training initiatives for district school boards or school authorities or consortia of boards/authorities in Northwestern Ontario.[47] Summer institutes were offered at Quetico Centre in August of 1998. Several years later, The Co-operative would turn over the remaining funds to the Northern Ontario Education Leaders [NOEL], a consortium representing a broader education spectrum.

Additional professional development was offered by The Co-operative, which had partnered with OISE, University of Toronto.[48] Conferences were held in December for trustees, supervisory officers, principals and secretary treasures. Conferences were held for teachers, principals and supervisory officers in February and in May for principals, secretary treasurers and supervisory officers. At the May conference, time was spent determining upcoming needs of participants so that conferences could be customized in the upcoming year.

The Ministry announced on September 4, 1998 that funding had been approved for an eight school venture through The Co-operative. That venture would provide for assistance in contract negotiations and the development of a shared accounting, financial report, human resources and payroll system.[49]

With the Ministry changing the funding model for school authorities, there was a need to deal with membership and services fees for member boards of The Co-operative. On April 13, 1999 Mike Del Nin, Business Administrator, prepared a paper titled Northwestern Ontario School Authorities and the Co-operative Services Program: Proposed Membership and Services Fee Models.[50] That document was circulated to member boards for their consideration and feedback. A final draft was to be submitted to the Board of Directors at a June board meeting for final consideration. On June 26th, 1999 the Board of Directors passed a resolution accepting the Service Fee Model and directed administration to proceed with implementation.

Back in 1998, The Co-operative entered into a contract with McEachern Marketing and Communications Limited to rename and rebrand The Co-operative. After considerable work, consultation and dialogue, the Program was renamed The Northern School Resource Alliance on October 1, 1999. In addition the NSRA (as it would come to be known) was re-branded.[51]

In January of 1999, The Co-operative entered into a contract with Sigma Systems to ready computers and servers for the Y2K issue. That was significant as the contract provided The Co-operative with work in all isolate schools in Northern Ontario.

In December of 1999, the NSRA entered into a contract with Science North to purchase, distribute, licence and use science kits for teachers and students. These kits were produced by Science North in both French and English. The French licence rights were eventually sold by the NSRA to the Ministry of Education for use in French speaking schools in Ontario.

On December 2, 1999 another associate member, The Hornepayne RCSS Board was approved effective September 1, 2000.

The NSRA had applied the Sigmoid Curve theory and prepared itself for the new millennium.

REFLECTIONS ON THE NORTHERN
SCHOOL RESOURCE ALLIANCE

Julie Roy-Ward, Secretary Treasurer
Hornepayne RCSS Board
Hornepayne, Ontario

What did the Co-operative mean to your local school?
The NSRA mean an entire network located in Northern Ontario
of peers, resources and local solutions.

Our local school was constantly up to date on Ministry
initiatives. Staff development was provided on current topics.
The technology aspect of our school was very well supported
because of staff (Co-op) knowledge and access to the service in
Northern Ontario.

**What impact did the Co-operative have upon your
community?**
The NSRA had a great influence on our community as the
benefits were locally known by such examples as: student
bursaries, installation of portable defibrillators in school and
student support via professionals for the testing of students.

Additional Memories That You Would Like to Share?
I loved the professional development which was grouped by
position. Not only were the presentation topics appropriate but
the groupings made for great peer support by sharing relevant
information.

CHAPTER TEN

The New Millennium Begins
(2000 – 2005)

As the NSRA entered the new millennium, several themes were evident at the Board and administrative level. First and foremost, it was imperative to continue to deliver quality services at affordable prices. There was continuing examination of the membership term and associated fees. Based on that, an organizational restructuring emerged. Incorporation was examined at the request of the Board of Directors. Current technology [IT] services were reviewed. Inter-regional school authority co-operation was discussed and by the end of 2005 the pending threat of further amalgamations to the school authorities and their co-operative was on the horizon.

Beginning in 2000, the member boards initiated a discussion on membership terms. The by-laws at the time provided for all members committing to a three year term. To withdraw, notice had to be given or membership would automatically renew. Due to the uncertainty of Ministry of Education funding (allocated on a one year basis) and the consideration of Summer Beaver DSA Board to withdraw, discussions arose about the feasibility of one year term membership.

On April 27, 2000 the following motion was tabled: That the term of membership be one (1) year renewable by January 31 of each year. The motion was defeated and the term of membership remained at three years.[52]

Then, on May 11, 2000 the Ministry of Education filed Ontario Regulation 280/00. That regulation provided for the amalgamation of three DSA Boards with much larger Boards. Specifically, Kashabowie DSA Board was amalgamated with The Lakehead Board; Sturgeon Lake DSA Board with Keewatin Patricia Board and Kilkenny with Superior Greenstone Board.[53] Two of these boards, Kashabowie and Sturgeon Lake, were members of the NSRA. Thus two members and their respective membership fees would withdraw as of January 1, 2001.

With the membership term resolved, it was time to find financial savings in order to keep membership fees affordable for the remaining members. In June of 2000, two things happened which triggered the restructuring process. a) At the June 28th Board of Directors' meeting, the resignation of Michael Del Nin, Business Administrator was presented to the Board from the Executive Committee. Trustees were advised that arrangements were being finalized with Ms. Erica Bailey to fill the position. b) Trustees were also advised that it was the intent of Fred Porter, CEO to retire on August 31, 2001 and in the interim, a succession plan was being prepared.

A consultant (Guy O'Brien, former Director of the Lakehead Separate School Board) was retained to assist the NSRA Board with the transition. After advertising for a new CEO and not finding a suitable candidate, the Board began discussion of restructuring the administration. On June 7, 2001 the following resolutions were passed: a) *"That the concept of restructuring be accepted."* b) *"That the Executive Committee pursue the restructuring plan as directed by the Board of Directors".*[54]

In keeping with that direction, the roles of CEO and Business Administrator were combined and assigned to Erica Bailey, effective September 1, 2001. To assist with that assignment, retiring CEO Fred Porter was contracted to mentor Erica Bailey, provide Supervisory Officer support, conference co-ordination, and professional growth and consulting support.

With the reorganization complete, the Board turned its attention to other matters. Over the next two years, the Board, in conjunction with legal counsel, examined the concept of incorporation of the NSRA instead of the current joint venture model.

The NSRA made application to the Ministry of Education to become an approved provider of professional learning programs. The approval of that application was announced to the Board in December of 2001.

During the spring of 2002, administration continued to examine the membership fee calculations. Consultation was carried out with member boards as to what they wanted to see in the way of membership fees.

In December of 2002 Erica Bailey provided an update to the Board on connectivity and technology. She reported that the Ministry of Education was supporting a pilot project in Summer Beaver for the use of a satellite technology to access the internet and possible video conferencing. This was being done with a view towards replacing expensive landline usage. From these initiatives was the creation of a Connectivity Committee comprised of trustees, principals, supervisory officers and Lo Endler, IT Consultant. The mandate of the Committee was to examine current connectivity and come up with recommendations for change/improvement.

2003 saw a focus on the finalization of membership fee policy and continued discussion of the concept of incorporation. On July 21, 2003 Erica Bailey presented the following member fee policy draft: a) The base calculation: *The fee shall be calculated as the prorated share of the average service fees as they would have been at the Member rates for the last three (3) years;* b) Provision for less than three years history and c) the Incentive Provision: *The current calculation may be revised (upon approval of the Board of Directors) for the first year of membership as an incentive to join NSRA".*

As a result the Board passed the following motion: That the Board of Directors approve the proposed policy "The Calculation".[55]

With regard to incorporation, the board requested Erica Bailey send out an information package to the Board members. In December of 2003 the Board tabled six questions regarding incorporation: a) What would be the annual ongoing costs of incorporation? b) Will this provide any better service to children by incorporating? c) Are we protected through insurance that the NSRA has, or at our own board? Are we getting any additional protection coverage? d) If incorporated, does the insurance fall solely on the Alliance? e) Have the supervisory officers been consulted regarding incorporation? f) Is the NSRA an entity that is recognized by the Ministry of Education? A motion to approve incorporation at the December 4, 2003 meeting was tabled in order to provide for supervisory officer consultation.

Education initiatives continued to play an important role for the NSRA. In June of 2003, Karen Walker accepted a half time contract as Project Officer for Students at Risk. Dorothy Nicholls was retained to provide workshops on "First Steps/ Oral Communications/Spelling and Writing". Jay Daiter was contracted with to co-ordinate the "Principal Mentoring - NSRA Member Boards Support Network". Susan Buchanan of Clarior Consulting was engaged to provide anti-bullying workshops for member schools.

Over the course of 2004, work continued on connectivity. Wardrop Engineering was contracted with to undertake a review. Recommendations from that review included upgrades in hardware, connectivity, software and training.

The Board continued to struggle with the issue of incorporation. In June of 2004 the Board established a Working

Committee. On December 2, 2004 the Working Committee reported to the Board. The Working Committee recommended to the Board of Directors to keep the joint venture as is and set up an arm's length (incorporated body) to look at outside activities. As a result the following motion was neither moved nor seconded and was declared dead: "That the Board of Directors approve incorporation of the NSRA to a Non-Profit Organization non share capital corporation as per attached documentation and information." A second motion, "That the Board of Directors approve the maintenance of NSRA Joint Venture organization for core business AND incorporate an arms length, non-share, non-profit organization for entrepreneurial activities for the purpose of supporting the school authorities" was defeated.

While the period of 2001-2004 was internally focused at the Board level, work was being done in the context of client development outside of Northwestern Ontario including Airy and Sabine DSA, Asquith-Garvey DSA, Foleyet DSA, Gogama DSA, James Bay Lowlands Secondary School Board, Moosonee DSA, Moosonee RCSS, Moose Factory DSA, Murchison and Lyell DSA. Conference attendance, particularly in the February sessions had increased from isolate schools, band operated schools, DSA boards and clients from outside of the region. By the end of 2004, conference revenues were netting approximately $30,000.00 per year. Education consulting was becoming more focused on student achievement and outcomes.

In addition, other parts of Northern Ontario were establishing co-operative models similar to the NSRA. Four school authorities in mid Northern Ontario formed the AGFM Co-operative (Asquith Garvey, Gogama, Foleyet and Missaranda DSA Boards). The English speaking school authorities outside of Northwestern Ontario formed the North Eastern Ontario School Authorities [NEOSA] and the French Language Authorities also formed a co-operative.

While this was exciting, a report to the Board of Directors in December 2005 indicated the results of a Freedom of Information request from the Ministry of Education regarding the future of school authorities in Ontario. While most of the information was redacted, one could infer from the list of documents provided that the school authorities were under scrutiny.

That would set the tone for the next few years and what was to occur in 2009.

REFLECTIONS ON THE NORTHERN
SCHOOL RESOURCE ALLIANCE

Teresa Larson, Secretary Treasurer
Atikokan RCSS Board
Atikokan, Ontario

What did the Co-operative mean to your local school?
The organization had a wealth of knowledge and expertise in which they shared with the small isolate school boards in Northern Ontario.

We were able to have access to many services and experts which we were not able to contract on our own due to limited funding. We were able to connect at local conferences held in Thunder Bay and share our thoughts and concerns with similar schools boards and schools.

It was a very effective Co-op which we were pleased to be part of…benefited teachers, staff and students. Professional development costs were shared. Legal fees were shared and legal services provided.

What impact did the Co-operative have upon your community?
The Co-op was able to bring in specialized persons to help assess the students at our school in order to give documentation to support funding of special education dollars which in turn helped the students with their learning. (i.e. special education equipment [kurzweil reader/laptop]/support [education assistant]

Additional Memories That You Would Like to Share?
The staff at the co-op were very experienced and knowledgeable. No matter how busy there were, they were always ready to help or assist when needed. Friendly, courteous staff. It was a pleasure working with them.

CHAPTER ELEVEN

Storm Clouds 2006 – 2009

As a result of continuing concerns about the future of school authorities, the Board of Directors requested administration to vigorously pursue information and assurance that political action was not imminent.

On January 27, 2006 Minister of Education Gerard Kennedy sent a letter to MPP Shelley Martel. In that letter, Minister Kennedy states: *"The government is not undertaking a review of school authorities at this time. If such a review were to take place, it would be done in consultation with our education stakeholders".*[56]

While that letter should have provided the reassurance that the Board wanted, rumours continued to abound that the future of school authorities were in jeopardy. Thus in the summer of 2006, a Freedom of Information request was filed for *"access to any/all documents prepared between December 16, 2005 to July 7, 2006 regarding future governance options regarding school authorities in Ontario. Information should include but it not limited to dissolution of amalgamation of school authorities in Ontario. Requesting also an Index of all documents in existence between these dates...."* When the government refused that request, the Information Privacy Commissioner was contacted and mediation was initiated.

In the spring of 2006 project funding was renewed. In place were Project Officers for Early Literacy (Dorothy Nicholls), MISA (Bill Ulrich), School Effectiveness (Devona Crowe), Special Education (Don Parsons) and Student Success Leader

(Wes Malo). All of these projects were to provide a very strong education focus upon student achievement and success over the next three years.

The Education and Project Officer Team: Devona Crow, School Effectiveness Leader with Ed Corbett, Project Officer

The Education and Project Officer Team: Don Parsons, Special Education

The Education and Project Officer Team:
Wes Malo, Student Success Leader

The Education and Project Officer Team:
Dororthy Nicholls, Early Literacy

In the interim, other events were unfolding at the Board of Directors and senior administration level. In the spring of 2006, Erica Bailey initiated discussion about the possibility of staff working from home and having a central meeting place. The idea was to reduce overhead and promote a new work model. As part of that strategy, a move was contemplated from the existing office in The Chapple Building to a classroom at Sherbrooke School. That move was initiated in the summer of 2006. However all was not well. The Board of Directors understood that the new office space was to house all staff and "the work at home model" was not approved. CEO Erica Bailey understood otherwise. The result was no walls, no privacy and staff with little room to work.

On September 8, 2006 the Board of Directors met to review correspondence from Erica Bailey indicating her desire to accept a position with the Kenora Catholic District School Board. The result was the passage of the following motion: *"That the Board of Directors accept, with regret, the resignation of Erica Bailey effective December 31, 2006 with a final day in office of October 13, 2006."* The Executive Committee also outlined a plan to fill the management of the NSRA. That plan included contracting with an academic supervisory officer as CEO to support the new financial officer.[57]

On October 11, 2006 The Board of Directors again met. The management plan outlined on September 8th by Executive Committee was implemented. The following resolutions were passed: *"That the Board of Directors approve the management restructuring of the Northern School Resource Alliance to include a 1.0 FTE Finance Officer and a .5 FTE Chief Executive Officer who is to be an Academic Supervisory Officer."* That the Board of Directors approve the Contract with Elaine Stewart as Finance Officer for the Northern School Resource Alliance." *"That the Board of Directors approve the appointment of Fred Porter as Chief*

Executive Officer for the Northern School Resource Alliance until August 31, 2008 at a rate of $500.00 per day for 120 days".[58]

The next few months were spent focusing on the transition to a new management team while continuing to emphasize the work of the project officers in the school authorities. Time was spent looking for a new workplace.

In December the Board of Directors again met. Hornepayne RCSS transferred its membership from NEOSA to the NSRA. The work of the Connectivity Committee was deemed complete and the Committee disbanded. Fred Porter reported on the most recent Freedom of Information request and the Board indicated political action would be needed to protect the school authorities.

December concluded with a move back to the original office at The Chapple Building so that staff could function more effectively in an office environment.

On February 20, 2007 the Ministry of Education, as a result of mediation decided to release information requested on the future governance options regarding school authorities in Ontario. Once again the key message from the Ministry was the following: "*The government has no plan to make changes in the governance of school authorities.*"[59]

In addition to the FOI requests, correspondence was shared by MPP's who had been contacted regarding the threat to school authorities. On April 3, 2007 Minister Kathleen Wynne wrote to MPP Michael Brown: "Let me assure you that the government is neither planning to eliminate nor amalgamate school authorities at this time." On April 17, 2007 MPP Bill Mauro wrote to John McInnis, Chair and Devona Crowe, Supervisory Officer of the Atikokan RCSS Board the following: "*The minister has assured me that our government is neither planning to eliminate nor amalgamate school authorities at this time.*"[60]

On May 3, 2007 Armand Giguere, Chair, Terry Swanson, Vice Chair, Fred Porter, CEO and Devona Crowe, Supervisory Officer for Atikokan RCSS met with MPP and Leader of the NDP, Howard Hampton. Howard Hampton (a former educator himself) said that "he is well aware we are doing a good job in giving an excellent education to the students in small communities".

On August 2, 2007 the Board of Directors met by teleconference. At that time the Board passed the following resolutions: *"That the Board of Directors accept, with regret, the resignation of Elaine Stewart effective August 31, 2007. That the Board of Directors approve the B&F Restructuring Plan on a trial basis (September 1- December 31, 2007 as presented (contract with Peter Stetsko, CA and Nora Kolmel, Secretary Treasurer of Red Lake RCSS) with a review at the December 2007 Annual General Meeting. That the contract of the CEO be extended until August 31, 2009."*

In the fall of 2007, Fred Porter began discussions with Emergency Medical Services and the Heart and Stroke Foundation regarding the provision of defibrillators for school authorities. Those discussions resulted in defibrillators being place in the member schools of Armstrong, Collins, Hornepayne, Nakina, Pickle Lake and Savant Lake. Staff training was also provided.

Project funding continued to flow to the NSRA for the member school authorities. The Council of Directors of Education provided $45,000 for special education. $25,977 was provided for the Learning to 18 project and $40,000 was allocated for the NOEL K-6 Literacy Project.

At the December 6, 2007 meeting, Fred Porter reported a return towards profitability. Mistakes in Financial Statements over the past several years were dealt with and the Bank approved the NSRA's line of credit, which was in jeopardy.

The services of Peter Stetsko and Nora Kolmel were continued until the end of February 2008, providing time to seek the services of a .5 FTE Financial Officer.

On May 6, 2008 the Board again met to deal with the management structure of the NSRA. The following resolutions were passed: "*That the Board of Directors approve the appointment of Fred Porter as CEO be continued for an additional three (3) year period, subject to arriving at an acceptable contract (September 1, 2008 –August 31, 2011 as recommended by Executive Committee.*" "*That the Board of Directors approve the appointment of Wes Malo, on a part-time basis, as an Assistant to the CEO, subject to arriving at an acceptable contract, (September 1, 2008-August 31, 2009), subject to renewal, as recommended by Executive Committee.*" "*That the Board of Directors approve the appointment of Doug Enstrom, on a part time basis, as Finance Officer subject to arriving at an acceptable contract (September 1, 2008 – August 31, 2009), subject to renewal, as recommended by the Executive Committee.*"[61]

With the management team issues resolved and project funding continued it seemed all was well. But it was not.

Despite the promise of the government, on June 4, 2008 the Ministry of Education made Regulation 178/08. The Mine Centre DSA Board was amalgamated with the Rainy River District School Board [DSB] without consultation. It appeared that this decision was based on the lobbying of nearby First Nations who believed tuition fees would be lower with Rainy River DSB than the Mine Centre DSA Board. In any event, that decision once again raised the spectre of the school authorities' demise.

At the December 4, 2008 annual general meeting, the Executive Committee reported to the Board of Directors about the possibility of incorporating a poison pill in the Letter of Agreement in the event of further amalgamations. Such a protective model was approved.

At that same meeting, Armand Gigure, Terry Swanson and Fred Porter reported on a meeting held with MPP Mike Gravelle about the future of school authorities. Mr. Gravelle indicated he had spoken to the Minister of Education who was aware of the situation but had not had time to get to the file. Mr. Gravelle stated that for the school authorities to do nothing was risky and an alternative model would give the Minister a way out. Mr. Gravelle indicated that he would embrace this. It was agreed that Fred Porter would provide a report to the school authorities with governance options for the boards to select for the Minister's consideration.

On the educational side, all schools now had videoconferencing equipment as well as at least one SMART board in each school. Early Literacy, headed by Dorothy Nicholls, provided for demonstration classrooms, an oral language project for the youngest students and early on-going intervention in co-operation with Northwestern Ontario District School Boards. School Effectiveness, headed by Devona Crowe, provided for new instruction strategies for teachers and review of best practices. Student Success, headed by Wes Malo, provided for a transition program for grade eight students having to leave their home communities to attend high school in a large city. Student Success also provided new resources and strategies for teachers of intermediate grades. Special Education, headed by Don Parsons, provided for identification supports as well as access to assessment and psychological services (The Ontario Psychological Association provided $100,000 to clear up the backlog of student assessments). Managing Information for Student Achievement, headed by Bill Ulrich, provided for the use of data and software to improve instructional strategies and thus student achievement. All of the projects were in support of Ministry of Education initiatives.

On the finance side, the NSRA had achieved a surplus; the first in several years. That surplus would be put into the NSRA reserve funds for future initiatives.

The NSRA moved into 2009 with some trepidation. During the spring a governance model option was selected and forwarded to the Minister. It provided for, in lieu of closure of small rural schools of DSA boards, the establishment of a school authority, which would allow the community to retain its small school.

On June 1, 2009 the promise made by a Minister of Education was broken and the isolate boards were betrayed.

REFLECTIONS ON THE NORTHERN
SCHOOL RESOURCE ALLIANCE

Laurie MacEachern, Principal
Holy Name of Jesus Catholic School
Hornepayne, Ontario

What did the Co-operative mean to your local school?
The NSRA provided extensive supports for our staff and students. The staff provided PD for staff on DRA, NOEL, OLA, School Effectiveness, WBTT, NTIP, critical literacy, boys' literacy, CODE, bully prevention, student assessments, character education and pathways. The staff provided ongoing support for administration. Monthly visits and supports were in place.

What impact did the Co-operative have upon your community?
The Co-operative was very well respected and welcomed in our community. The Co-operative explored various avenues to successfully support our staff and students. Our grade 3 and 6 EQAO scores were always above provincial standards due to the supports from the Co-operative. Staff were comfortable inviting the Co-operative to visit our school and support the staff where needed.

Additional Memories That You Would Like to Share?
The personal touch and sincereness was always appreciated.

CHAPTER TWELVE

A Promise Betrayed
June 2009 – August 2009

Program Support Officer Dorothy Kostreba was notified of a June 1ˢᵗ 1:30pm teleconference for the CEO Fred Porter (in his capacity of Supervisory Officer for the English Section of the Hornpanye RCSS Board, Nakina DSA Board and Northern DSA Board) with Dawna Johnson, Regional Manager of the Northwestern Ontario Ministry of Education Regional Office. Also on that teleconference was Kevin Debnam, Supervisory Officer of the Atikokan RCSS Board and Red Lake Combined RCSS Board and Joanne Debnam, Supervisory Officer of the French Section of the Hornepayne RCSS Board.

Dorothy Kostreba, Program Support Officer

Dawna Johnson announced the amalgamation of a number of school authorities, by Regulation 486/01 would occur effective September 1, 2009. She further indicated that there would be interim restrictions regarding hiring, promoting and spending outlined in that regulation. She advised that letters would be forthcoming to chairs from the Minister and to supervisory officers from the Deputy Minister later in the day. Finally, Dawna Johnson advised of a teleconference on Tuesday at 3:15pm with the Minister and chairs of effected boards and school authorities and at 4:30pm with the Assistant Deputy Minister, directors of education and supervisory officers. Later in the day the promised letters appeared by email.[62]

A press release by the Ministry of Education indicated that 20 of the 24 school authorities in Ontario were being amalgamated with district school boards.[63] The press release indicated, "*Students and teachers from the small school authorities often don't have access to the same resources and supports as their counterparts at larger district school boards, resulting in below average student achievement. This new structure will increase support for Aboriginal students and will give all teachers and students greater access to the tools and resources they need to succeed and help improve student achievement.*" The press release also indicated that the Ministry of Education was currently holding consultations with the three school authorities in the lower James Bay area.

That information was re-iterated the next day on the teleconference by the Minister. When challenged about the issue of student achievement, the Minister simply stated that history would be the judge. (The interesting aside to this matter is due to the size of the student samples in school authorities, the Education Quality and Accountability Office does not make public grade 3 and 6 testing results. Thus the matter of student achievement was unable to be debated in public).

Assistant Deputy Minister Raymond Theberge provided the same information to the Directors of Education and Supervisory Officers. However no opportunity for questions was provided.

The next few weeks saw personnel focus on the transition issues. Letters were sent to parents signed by the Director of Education of the receiving DSB and the Supervisory Officer of the school authority. Meetings were held with school authority personnel and supervisory officers to deal with questions about the transition. Issues raised included job security and seniority, loss of jobs in small communities, continuing parental input into local school governance and first nation representation at the governance level.

Fred Porter also met with the NSRA Staff to deliver the announcement. Issues raised included job loss, the need to deal with a collective agreement that had not been renegotiated and transition logistics.

There was a growing anger about the heavy-handed manner in which the Ministry of Eduation had behaved. In an open letter to Premier Dalton McGuinty and Education Minster Kathleen Wynne, George Seaton, Chair of Connell and Ponsford DSA Board stated: *"Your recent action of amalgamating some 19 school authorities with other boards, without any due process or consultation with communities, parents and trustees, is not acceptable in a supposed democratic society. This decision was made by people who did not grace us with their presence, do not know our school or community. It takes away jobs, affects our children, local autonomy and long-term health and quality of life in our community."*[64]

By the time the Board of Directors of the NSRA met on July 30, 2009 a strategy had emerged for dealing with the amalgamation. The recommendation was outlined as follows: *"Letter to the Minister recommending an alternative amalgamation arrangement (amalgamation of Catholic School Authorities into one or two DSB's and similar amalgamation of Public School Authorities into two DSB's). In the absence of same, pursuit of an injunction to halt amalgamations and the request of a Judicial Review of the Minister's actions (with an emphasis on the lack of due process and the fact there is full ongoing consultation in the Moosonee area).*" With the strategy clear, the following resolution was passed: "That the Board of Directors authorize access to the NSRA Reserve Funds for the purpose of funding a judicial review of the Minister's decision to amalgamate School Authorities with District School Boards."

On August 6, 2009 a letter, signed by Armand Giguere, Chair of the NSRA and Terry Swanson, Vice-Chair of the NSRA was sent to Minister Wynne. That letter requested a one-year suspension of the amalgamation and during that time, an opportunity to explore the possibility of merging with other school authorities (mirroring the same opportunity presented by the Minister to the school authorities in lower James Bay). The letter also went on to state that in the absence of an affirmative response, the NSRA intended to seek an order halting or suspending the amalgamations, pending a judicial review of the government's actions.[65]

On August 14, the Minster's response was received. While she noted the request, the response simply indicated, "*transition teams are in place to support the amalgamation effective September 1, 2009 and will remain to support boards as long as necessary*".[66]

What the letter did not say was that Ontario Regulation 309/09 was made on August 12, 2009 and filed on August 14th. The pertinent piece of that regulation for the school authorities was the following: "*Despite subsection (1) on September 1, 2009, the financial obligations of boards in respect of membership in the Northern School Resource Alliance are transferred to the Lakehead District School Board, to be held in trust by it on behalf of such boards"* and *"On or after September 1, 2009, the Lakehead District School Board shall ensure that the Northern School Resource Alliance provides services to the board for which financial obligations were transferred under subsection (s) until the services are no longer required, at which time the Lakehead District School Board shall wind up the Northern School Resource Alliance."*

Not only had the government betrayed its promise to consult prior to contemplating amalgamation but had ensured that its decision was not going to be reviewed by a judge. The funds that the NSRA had in its reserve fund ($863,318.00 which had been earned through project work, etc, and which had not been granted by the Ministry of Education) was no longer under the control of the NSRA.

On August 27, 2009 a final attempt last-ditch attempt to stop the amalgamation and save the school authorities was made. A letter of complaint was sent to the Office of the Ontario Ombudsman.[67] No formal response was ever received although a phone call to Armand Giguere, Chairperson indicated that the matter fell outside the Ombudsman's jurisdiction.

On August 31, 2009 a final Board of Director meeting was held by teleconference. That final business for the Board was a resolution to approve the contract negotiated with NSRA CUPE staff.

The end of the school authorities and the NSRA had come to a close. A Toronto based Minister had prevailed over education and co-operation in the small school authorities of Northwestern Ontario. All that was left to do was the transition to closure.

REFLECTIONS ON THE NORTHERN
SCHOOL RESOURCE ALLIANCE

Anglea Miller, Principal
Nakina Public School
Nakina, Ontario

What did the Co-operative mean to your local school?

The Co-operative was our life line to education. It helped bring together people/teachers from diverse communities and provided them with opportunities. The professional development opportunities were incredible and have had nothing comparable since. The resources we were allocated were amazing. The Co-operative put us in the forefront with technology and our students were always first.

What impact did the Co-operative have upon your community?

Having the Board located in our community with members from Nakina had a huge impact. Local governance was crucial in sharing the message of the school. Parent representatives shared information with other parents. Just knowing the people who made up the Board was important and is sadly missed.

Having a school in the community with the resources to keep them at par with the province was appreciated.

Additional Memories That You Would Like to Share?

Having project managers available to us throughout the year to assist us with curriculum, administration issues was amazing and something I really miss. Having technology that worked and being trusted with equipment was very special.

CHAPTER THIRTEEN

Over Before Its Time!

September 1, 2009 saw the beginning of the end of the NSRA. While Fred Porter remained in the role of CEO for the remaining months of the NSRA's existence, all expenditures required the prior approval of Kathy Pozihun, Superintendent of Business and Treasurer of the Lakehead District School Board.

During the next few months, staff of the NSRA provided transitional support to the DSBs that had inherited the school authorities. Payroll and human resource services were transitioned as was IT support. This ensured an orderly transition for the staff of the school authorities.

The school authorities were now under the supervision of the DSB to which each had been amalgamated. Ahead of them were many issues to be addressed such as principal contracts, staffing issues, the fate of secretary treasurers, and the continuation of existing programs (such as full time Junior and Senior Kindergarten). Many of those issues would not be clear until well into the end of the 2009-2010 school year and beyond.

File archives were sorted, logged and shipped off to the DSBs. Files for long ago closed isolate school boards were logged and sent to the Ministry of Education Regional Office for archival.

Staff at the NSRA were laid off in a staggered fashion as the work of transitioning and closing slowed down. Near the end of March 2010 a public auction was held to dispose of all remaining physical assets.

On March 31, 2010 the remaining staff of the NSRA met for one last time. Wes Malo, Student Success Leader, Connie Andrea, Senior Accounting Clerk and Fred Porter, CEO stood in an empty office. There was no more to do and little to say. The Ministry of Education had said in its press release that the larger school boards would do more for students and teachers of the school authorities. On that last morning, it was difficult to believe that big was better

Fred Porter

REFLECTIONS ON THE NORTHERN
SCHOOL RESOURCE ALLIANCE

Nora Kolmel, Secretary Treasurer (with input from Suzanne Chartier-White (Principal) and Vaughn Blab(Trustee))
Red Lake Combined RCSS Board
Red Lake, Ontario

What did the above named Co-operative mean to your local school?

Being part of the Co-operative gave the school access to expertise that a small isolate school would not have been able to afford or contact. When we did not have a principal, a secondment was provided. When consultants were required, arrangements were made to pool resources to the needs of the school, i.e.- special education, speech pathology, IT purchasing, maintenance and instruction of programs.

The co-operative was a lifeline for the principal in the school; principals had opportunities to compare situations/problems and how to address them. The people working for the co-operative were dedicated; collectively they had the expertise and experience that allowed no waste of time getting experience for the activities. They were a good buffer for the Ministry (of Education) initiatives that were designed for large boards with teams to meet the demands where an isolate school would not have the human resources. Professional development was taken care of by the NSRA with more support, initiatives were filtered to meet the demands of a small school with multi grade classrooms, show how to make learning happen. Dorothy (Kostreba) gave her 'heart and soul' to the organization, did a grand job working behind the scenes for the PD arrangements; details were attended to and always with a smile.

The school staff was provided up to date information and teaching techniques so that the students would advance seamlessly. As the demands from the Ministry grew, the workload grew heavier and the human resources did not. The NSRA took a lot of the weight and reporting demands. We did not lose students to the neighbouring schools for lack of confidence in our school.

What impact did the Co-operative have upon your community?

I am not sure if the community of Red Lake knew of the organization's support to the local school and staff. Most communities take notice if something is not running properly and that did not happen. We had the addition to the school, local community support for a full size gym in the school. The community of Ear Falls created a school board and joined the school in Red Lake. The French language school was formed with assistance from the expertise of the supervisory office Maurice Tremblay of the Board. The Trustees were strong on local autonomy, participated similarly to parent council, and worked for the school and for the school needs versus basically reviewers of policy.

Additional Memories That you Would Like to Share.

My education and experience grew by working with the people of the Co-operative. Initially the shared financial service was a 'back office administrative function', data entry and monthly reports for the Board. It was a support service and a review level for my work in the office and reconciliation. When I started we were working manually, cheques, typing recording purchase orders and accounting projects. With the introduction of computers and accounting software – there was a learning curve. The professional development was current and timely – aspects of the education were useful right away. New ministry accounts and reporting requirements initiated new training opportunities. I could call any other person within the organization for assistance – Capital grant plan reporting during the construction phases, developing budgets within the Ministry's Isolate Board guidelines, Pay Equity, Employment Equity, Social Contract and negotiations during difficult budget cutting times.

Four events stand out for me: Getting called to Thunder Bay to meet with Guy O'Brien, our Supervisory Officer, and Fred Porter, Director of the Northern School Resource Alliance – regarding further budget cuts due to declining enrolments. Both men acknowledged the work I had been doing over a period of years of tightening the budget and spending, they knew that there were no further cuts that could be done other than staffing. They needed me to accept that fact. When asked how I felt coming to Thunder Bay – my reply was 'like driving to my own hanging'. Affecting staff was the last resort and I needed help with that.

Secondly – a trip to a fly-in school board to assist with setting up the Board office. We flew in a plane (with more duct tape use than I've ever seen) to a one-room school with one teacher. A beautiful location but I received an instant education of the differences in arranging for supplies and services for a fly-in remote location. The entire office had to be set up, desk, IT, files, contacts, and training on using the software. There was nothing left from the predecessor to find past information. Winter was coming and arrangements for fuel, power-everything had to be done immediately. Training the new secretary treasurer was minimal but enough to get started, then the contact was by phone. The NSRA staff had that information and the experience how to guide the transition from one person to another – so that the school children would not be affected.

Thirdly, I had been in the hospital and shortly after that had to go on jury duty. The finance/payroll was done through the co-operative office staff, T4's as this was year-end, and audit was being done while I was out in Kenora on jury duty. Phone contact was all we had, in the evenings after court was recessed. Mike (Del Nin) was in my office – locating the information and gathering the auditors' questions for me to answer in the evenings. I always was confident that the office would be able to continue in the event I was away or replaced, the co-op was readily available and was instrumental in engaging the people with the needed skill sets to get the job done. I learned to LISTEN to the messages and to READ the fine print in documents, memorandums, and the context of the wording of paragraphs and not skim.

We had the attitude: how can we do this with the resources we have? It was a positive atmosphere to work in, respecting the differences in our communities, school, and geographic areas. Over time, it felt a bit like family. When a NSRA finance clerk proposed working from a home office via the computer system - so that she could stay with her baby and still work, I was asked if I would be willing to participate in this project. I found that pilot was successful; now a satellite office is more commonplace.

Fourth but not last – the importance of contracts. When the sudden announcement of amalgamation of the isolate boards to district services boards, loss of my own position and the dismantling of the consortium, the order of business was contracts. Over the years, the Board had contracts for shared services, legal services, purchases, transportation, IT services, contracts with the consortium and with principal and administrative senior staff.

The networking and teamwork with secretary treasurers, Principals, Supervisory officers, Trustees, Ministry personnel, the co-operative staff; all helped me be the person/employee I am today.

ADDENDUM ONE

Member Isolate Boards/School Authorities of the Northern School Resource Alliance

and

Their Schools

Atikokan R.C.S.S. Board:

The Atikokan RCSS Board was the school authority board for St. Patrick's School. It is located in Atikokan, approximately 208 kilometers (just off Highway 11) from the Northern School Resource Alliance. Below are photographs of the two old schools and the new school which was officially opened on November 1, 2001.

Collins DSA Board:

The Collins DSA Board was the school authority board for Bernier-Stokes Public School. It is located in Collins approximately 300 kilometers from the Northern School Resource Alliance. It is accessible only by railway year round, snowmobile by winter and float/ski plane.

Below is an aerial photograph of Collins, as well as photographs of Bernier-Stokes School being built by a local work force and a photograph of the finished school.

Caramat DSA Board:

The Caramat DSA Board was the school authority board for Caramat Public School. It is located in Caramat approximately 360 kilometers from the Northern School Resource Alliance (just off Highway 625).

Below is a photograph of the most recently constructed school which was originally built in 1962 and added on to in 1983.

Connell and Ponsford DSA Board:

The Connell and Ponsford DSA Board was the school authority board for Crolancia Public School. It is located in Pickle Lake approximately 530 kilometers from the Northern School Resource Alliance (just off Highway 599). The name Crolancia Public School comes from the towns of Pickle Crow ('CRO'), Pickle Lake-Pickle Landing ('LAN') and Central Patricia ('CIA').

Below is a photograph of the most recently constructed school that was opened in the spring of 1981.

Ignace RCSS Board:

The Ignace RCSS Board was the school authority board for Immaculate Conception School. It is located in Ignace approximately 250 kilometers from the Northern School Resource Alliance (just off Highway 17).

Below is a photograph of the current school.

Kashabowie DSA Board:

The Kashabowie DSA Board was the school authority board for Kashabowie Public School. It is located in Kashabowie approximately 114 kilometers from the Northern School Resource Alliance (just off Highway 11). In the fall of 2000 the board was amalgamated with the Lakehead District School Board.

Below is a photograph of the current school.

Mine Centre DSA Board:

The Mine Centre DSA Board was the school authority board for Mine Centre Public School. It is located in Mine Centre approximately 300 kilometers from the Northern School Resource Alliance (just off Highway 11).

Below is a photograph of the current school.

Hornepayne R.C.S.S. Board:

The Hornepayne RCSS Board was the school authority board for Holy Name of Jesus School/Ecole Holy Name of Jesus School. It is located in Hornepayne approximately 500 kilometers from the Northern School Resource Alliance (just off Highway 631). The school provided for an English language program and a French language program.

Below is a photograph of the current school.

Nakina DSA Board:

The Nakina DSA Board was the school authority board for Nakina Public School. It is located in Nakina approximately 350 kilometers from the Northern School Resource Alliance (just off Highway 594). Nakina Public School and St. Brigid School shared a gymnasium for combined use, the first such combined school in Ontario.

Below is a photograph of the current school.

Photo of the combined Nakina Public School and St. Bridgid School.

Northern DSA Board:

The Northern DSA Board was the school Authority board for Armstrong Public School and Savant Lake Public School. Armstrong is located 250 kilometers from the Northern School Resource Alliance (just off Highway 527). Savant Lake Public school is located approximately 373 kilometers from the Northern School Resource Alliance (just off Highway 599)

Below are photographs of the current school.

Red Lake Combined RCSS Board:

The Red Lake Combined RCSS Board was the school authority board for St. John's Catholic School. It is located in Red Lake approximately 580 kilometers from the Northern School Resource Alliance (just off Highway 105). The school services the communities of Red Lake, Madsen, Balmertown, Cochenour, McKenzie Island and Ear Falls.

Below is a photograph of the current school.

Summer Beaver DSA Board:

The Summer Beaver DSA Board was the school authority board for Nibinamik Education Centre. It is located in Summer Beaver approximately 470 kilometers from the Northern School Resource Alliance. It is accessible by air year round and winter road during the winter months.

Below are photographs of the original school as well as the current school.

Upsala DSA Board:

The Upsala DSA Board was the school authority board for Upsala Public School. It is located in Upsala approximately 150 kilometers from the Northern School Resource Alliance (on Highway 17).

Below is a photograph of the current school.

ADDENDUM TWO

Elected Trustees on the Board of Directors of the Northern School Resource Alliance

and

Senior Administration

DECEMBER 1994

Chairperson:	Terry Swanson (Nakina DSA Board)
Vice Chairperson:	Ed Morrissette (Atikokan RCSS Board)
Executive Committee:	Teresa Van Dusen (Red Lake Combined RCSS Board)
	Bert Johnson (Upsala DSA Board)
	Don Sofea (Summer Beaver DSA Board)
Trustees:	Sylvie Gilbert (Ignace RCSS Board)
	Carol Groves (Sturgeon Lake DSA Board)
	Raymond Lelievre (Caramat DSA Board)
	Irene Mayo (Kashabowie DSA Board)
	Peter Patience (Collins DSA Board)
	Elsie Sakakeesic (Slate Falls DSA Board)
	George Seaton (Connell & Ponsford DSA Board)
	Larry Sweigard (Mine Centre DSA Board)
Chief Executive Officer:	Fred Porter
Business Administrator:	Mike Del Nin

DECEMBER 1995

Chairperson:	Terry Swanson (Nakina DSA Board)
Vice Chairperson:	Ed Morrissette (Atikokan RCSS Board)
Executive Committee:	Teresa Van Dusen (Red Lake Combined RCSS Board)
	Bert Johnson (Upsala DSA Board)
	Don Sofea (Summer Beaver DSA Board)
Trustees:	Carol Groves (Sturgeon Lake DSA Board)
	Don Hyatt (Mine Centre DSA Board)
	Raymond Lelievre (Caramat DSA Board)
	Leona Masakeyash (Slate Falls DSA Board)
	Irene Mayo (Kashabowie DSA Board)
	George Seaton (Connell & Ponsford DSA Board)
	Doris Therrien (Ignace RCSS Board)
	Mike Yellowhead (Collins DSA Board)
Chief Executive Officer:	Fred Porter
Business Administrator:	Mike Del Nin

97

DECEMBER 1996

Chairperson:	Terry Swanson (Nakina DSA Board)
Vice Chairperson:	Ed Morrissette (Atikokan RCSS Board)
Executive Committee:	Bert Johnson, (Upsala DSA Board)
	Bev Kondra (Dryden RCSS Board)
	Marie Warren (Atikokan Board of Education)
Trustees:	Ruby Bighead (Slate Falls DSA Board & Slate Falls First Nation)
	Armand Giguere (Caramat DSA Board)
	Carol Groves (Sturgeon Lake DSA Board)
	Don Hyatt (Mine Centre DSA Board)
	Irene Mayo (Kashabowie DSA Board)
	Roger Oskineegish (Summer Beaver DSA Board)
	Gerald Rousseau (Fort Frances-Rainy River RCSS Board)
	George Seaton (Connell & Ponsford DSA Board)
	Doris Therrien (Ignace RCSS Board)
	Teresa Van Dusen (Red Lake Combined RCSS Board)
	Mike Yellowhead (Collins DSA Board)
Chief Executive Officer:	Fred Porter
Business Administrator:	Mike Del Nin

JANUARY 1998 (In lieu of December 1997)

Chairperson:	Terry Swanson (Nakina DSA Board)
Vice Chairperson:	Ed Morrissette (Atikokan RCSS Board)
Executive Committee:	Armand Giguere (Caramat DSA Board)
	Don Sofea (Summer Beaver DSA Board)
	Teresa Van Dusen (Red Lake Combined RCSS Board)
Trustees:	Eli Albany (Collins DSA Board)
	Roland Baril (Ignace RCSS Board)
	Cheryl Dane (Northern DSA Board)
	Kim Dennis (Mine Centre DSA Board)
	Roger Fobister (Grassy Narrows First Nation)
	Carol Groves (Sturgeon Lake DSA Board)
	Cheryl Lovisa (Northwest Catholic District School Board)
	Irene Mayo (Kashabowie DSA Board)
	Gordon McBride (Rainy River District School Board)
	Barb Nelson (Upsala DSA Board)
	George Seaton (Connell and Ponsford DSA Board)
Chief Executive Officer:	Fred Porter
Business Administrator:	Mike Del Nin

99

DECEMBER 1998

Chairperson:	Terry Swanson (Nakina DSA Board)
Vice Chairperson:	Ed Morrissette (Atikokan RCSS Board)
Executive Committee:	Armand Giguere (Caramat DSA Board)
	Eva Peters (Upsala DSA Board)
	Linda Pickett (Connell & Ponsford DSA Board)
Trustees:	Eli Albany (Collins DSA Board)
	Bonnie Atlookan (Summer Beaver DSA Board)
	Roland Baril (Ignace RCSS Board)
	Cheryl Dane (Northern DSA Board)
	Kim Dennis (Mine Centre DSA Board)
	Carol Groves (Sturgeon Lake DSA Board)
	Cheryl Lovisa (Northwest Catholic District School Board)
	Irene Mayo (Kashabowie DSA Board)
	Gordon McBride (Rainy River District School Board)
	Colleen Swain (Grassy Narrows First Nation)
	Teresa Van Dusen (Red Lake Combined RCSS Board)
Chief Executive Officer:	Fred Porter
Business Administrator:	Mike Del Nin

100

DECEMBER 1999

Chairperson:	Terry Swanson (Nakina DSA Board)
Vice Chairperson:	Armand Giguere (Caramat DSA Board)
Executive Committee:	Ed Morrissette (Atikokan RCSS Board)
	Eva Peters (Upsala DSA Board)
	Brian Robertson (Connell & Ponsford DSA Board)
Trustees:	Eli Albany (Collins DSA Board)
	Roland Baril (Ignace RCSS Board)
	Carol Groves (Sturgeon Lake DSA Board)
	Richard Koski (Northern DSA Board)
	Nel Laur (Mine Centre DSA Board)
	Irene Mayo (Kashabowie DSA Board)
	Raymond Sugarhead (Summer Beaver DSA Board)
	Teresa Van Dusen (Red Lake Combined RCSS Board
Chief Executive Officer:	Fred Porter
Business Administrator:	Mike Del Nin

DECEMBER 2000

Chairperson:	Terry Swanson (Nakina DSA Board)
Vice Chairperson:	Armand Giguere (Caramat DSA Board)
Executive Committee:	Eva Peters (Upsala DSA Board)
	Brian Robertson (Connell & Ponsford DSA Board)
	Marie Warren (Rainy River District School Board)
Trustees:	Eli Albany (Collins DSA Board)
	Kim Dennis (Mine Centre DSA Board)
	Michel Gauthier (Red Lake Combined RCSS Board)
	Carol Groves (Sturgeon Lake DSA Board)
	Caroloyn Homonko (Kashabowie DSA Board)
	Lennie Markwick (Northern DSA Board)
	Ed Morrissette (Atikokan RCSS Board)
	Kathleen Toutant (Ignace RCSS Board)
Chief Executive Officer:	Fred Porter
Business Administrator:	Erica Bailey

DECEMBER 2002

Chairperson:	Armand Giguere (Caramat DSA Board)
Vice Chairperson:	Nel Laur (Mine Centre DSA Board)
Executive Committee:	Garry Gustafson (Northern DSA Board)
	George Seaton (Connell & Ponsford DSA Board)
	Marie Warren (Atikokan RCSS Board
Trustees:	Bert Cook (Collins DSA Board)
	Catherine Hutchison (Red Lake Combined RCSS Board)
	Eva Peters (Upsala DSA Board)
	Terry Swanson (Nakina DSA Board)
	Michel Trudel (Ignace RCSS Board)
Chief Executive Officer:	Erica Bailey

DECEMBER 2003

Chairperson:	Armand Giguere (Caramat DSA Board)
Vice Chairperson:	Nel Laur (Mine Centre DSA Board)
Executive Committee:	John McInnis (Atikokan RCSS Board)
	George Seaton (Connell & Ponsford DSA Board)
	Terry Swanson (Nakina DSA Board)
Trustees:	Diane Laybourne (Northern DSA Board)
	Catherine Hutchison (Red Lake Combined RCSS Board)
	Rene Nadeau (Ignace RCSS Board)
	Caroline Paavola (Collins DSA Board)
	Eva Peters (Upsala DSA Board)
	Lisa Yellowhead (Summer Beaver DSA Board)
Chief Executive Officer:	Erica Bailey

DECEMBER 2004

DECEMBER 2005

Chairperson: Terry Swanson (Nakina DSA Board)

Vice Chairperson: John McInnis (Atikokan RCSS Board)

Executive
Committee: Armand Giguere (Caramat DSA Board)

                        Colleen Hyatt (Mine Centre DSA Board)

                        George Seaton (Connell & Ponsford DSA
                            Board)

Trustees: Diane Laybourne (Northern DSA Board)

                        Eva Peters (Upsala DSA Board)

                        Teresa Van Dusen (Red Lake Combined
                            RCSS Board)

                        Lisa Yellowhead (Summer Beaver DSA
                            Board)

Chief Executive   Erica Bailey
Officer:

DECEMBER 2006

Chairperson:	Armand Giguere (Caramat DSA Board)
Vice Chairperson:	Terry Swanson (Nakina DSA Board)
Executive Committee:	Colleen Hyatt (Mine Centre DSA Board)
	John McInnis (Atikokan RCSS Board)
	George Seaton (Connell & Ponsford DSA Board)
Trustees:	Michelle Fortier (Ignace RCSS Board)
	Jenna Gonyou (Upsala DSA Board)
	Dennis Mackie (Hornepayne RCSS Board)
	Jonathon Spade (Collins DSA Board)
	Judy Turner (Northern DSA Board)
	Teresa Van Dusen (Red Lake Combined RCSS Board)
Chief Executive Officer:	Fred Porter
Business Administrator:	Elaine Stewart

DECEMBER 2007

Chairperson: Armand Giguere (Caramat DSA Board)

Vice Chairperson: Terry Swanson (Nakina DSA Board)

Executive Committee: Colleen Hyatt (Mine Centre DSA Board)

John McInnis (Atikokan RCSS Board)

George Seaton (Connell & Ponsford DSA Board)

Trustees: Michelle Fortier (Ignace RCSS Board)

Juerg Gees (Collins DSA Board)

Jenna Gonyou (Upsala DSA Board)

Dennis Mackie (Hornepayne RCSS Board)

Judy Turner (Northern DSA Board)

Teresa Van Dusen (Red Lake Combined RCSS Board)

Chief Executive Officer: Fred Porter

Bibliography

Education Improvement Commission. The Road Ahead. 1977

Jones, Reg et al. A Review of Services Provided by the Service Unit of the Umfreville District School Area Board. 1998

Krezonoski, Bill. Examining the Characteristics and Components of Educational Co-operatives. August 1996.

Ontario Ministry of Education. Special Report Small School Boards in Northwestern Ontario in the Years 1966 to 1977. December 1977.

Ontario Ministry of Education and Training. Report on Educational Services Issues In Northern Ontario. 1994.

Rousseau, Bruce. Co-operative Services Unit: A Case Study. July 19, 1984.

Porter, Fred. The Umfreville District School Area Board Pilot Project. July 31, 1990.

Endnotes

[1] Memorandum to Public and Separate School Inspectors in Areas 1, 2, 3 from A.H. McKague, Superintendent of Supervision, Ontario Department of Education Re: Assistance to Isolated Elementary Schools. (April 1, 1996)

[2] Memo to Dr. J. R. McCarthy from R.R. Steele Regional Director of Ontario Ministry of Education re Administration of Isolated Schools. (March 18, 1970)

[3] School Business Administration in Region 1 by Staff of School Business Administration in Northwestern Ontario. (April 1972)

[4] A Review in Depth of the Current Status of Northern Corp Schools and Other Isolated Schools in Northwestern Ontario by W.M. Ransberry, Chairman, J.A. Martin, Secretary and J.L. Duchesneau. (1973)

[5] Memorandum to Directors of Education, Superintendents of Separate Schools and Re-organization of The Regional Service of the Ministry of Education by E.E. Stewart, Deputy Minister of Education. (November 16, 1973)

[6] Memorandum to Regional Directors of Education from H.K. Fisher, Assistant Deputy Minister of Education. (December 27, 1974)

[7] Memorandum to J. Martin, Director of School Business and Finance Branch from P.E. Workman, Superintendent of Business and Finance, Northwestern Ontario Region. (October 14, 1976)

[8] Isolate Board Staffing Plan Co-operative Management Services. (September 21, 1976)

[9] Staffing Schedule and Proposed Budget

[10] Minutes Umfreville District School Area Board Meeting. (November 26, 1976)

11   Memorandum to P.E. Workman, Superintendent of Business and Finance from R.R. Steele, Regional Director of Edcuation. (December 20, 1976)

12   School Management Services 1977 Budget Office Operation

13   Memorandum to File from R.R. Steele re Isolate Boards – School Management Services. (March 23, 1977)

14   The Co-operative Services Unit to serve Isolate and Small Local Boards in Northwestern Ontario (For Study by Trustees) Issued by the Regional Director Northwestern Ontario Region Ministry of Education. (March 1981)

15   Summary of Recommendations from A Review of Services Provided by The Service Unit of The Umfreville District School Area Board by Reg Jones et all. (1988)

16   Draft Letter of Agreement between Supervisory Officer of an Isolate Board and Director of Education for Umfreville. (1989)

17   Meeting Dates/Agenda Topics of Umfreville District School Area Board Advisory Committee. (1989/1990)

18   Memorandum to Chairpersons, Principals, Secretary-Treasurers of Isolate School Boards by M. Twomey, Regional Director of Education. (June 20, 1989)

19   Summary of Recommendations from the Umfreville District School Area Board Pilot Project Report. (July 31, 1990)

20   Meeting of Umfreville Advisory Committee. (June 5, 1990)

21   Meeting of Umfreville Advisory Committee. (October 12, 1990)

22   Letter to T. Swanson, Chairman Umfreville Advisory Committee from Marion Boyd, Minister of Education. (November 30, 1990)

23   Letter to J. Whicher, Director of Education of Umfreville District School Area Board from J. Dojack, Regional Director of Education. (March 25, 1991)

24   Response of the Umfreville Advisory Committee to the Ministry of Education as set forth in the Regional Directors Letter of March 25, 1991.

25   Letter to J. Whicher, Director of Education of Umfreville District School Area Board from J. Dojack, Regional Director of Education. (April 29, 1991)

26   Excerpt from Minutes of Umfreville Advisory Committee. (December 6, 1993)

27   Excerpt from the Ontario Ministry of Education Project Unit Report. (1994)

28   Letter to Chairpersons, Northwestern Ontario Isolate Boards from J. Dojack, Regional Director of Education. (May 28, 1993)

29   Letter to A. Gouriluk, Chairperson Umfreville District School Area Board from J. Dojack, Regional Director of Edcuation. (August 16, 1993)

30   Minutes of Teleconference Isolate Board Chairs. (September 28, 1993)

31   Organizational Structure of The Northwestern Ontario School Boards' Co-operative Services Program. (1994)

32   Funding Mechanisms of The Northwestern Ontario School Boards' Co-operative Services Program. (1994)

33   Minutes of Meeting of the Northwestern Ontario School Boards' Co-operative Services Program. (May 6, 1994)

34   Letter to J. Dojack, Regional Director of Education from J. Whicher, Director of Education. (May 10, 1994)

35   Chief Executive Officer Performance Objectives. (November 18, 1994)

36   Draft Mission Statement from the 1994 Annual Report of Chief Executive Officer. (1994)

37   The Northwestern Ontario School Boards' Co-operative Services Program Fact Sheet. (1994)

38   Excerpt from Ontario Ministry of Education of Northwestern Regional Office Funding Guidelines. (1994)

39   The Northwestern Ontario School Boards' Co-operative Services Program Financial Statements for the Period Ended December 31, 2994.

40   The Northwestern Ontario School Boards' Co-operative Services Program Annual Report. (1995)

41   The Northwestern Ontario School Boards' Co-operative Services Program Annual Report. (1996)

42   Excerpt from The Road Ahead by Education Improvement Commission. (August 1997)

43   Excerpt from http://vannervarblogspot.ca regarding the Sigmoid Curve. (2009)

44   The Northwestern Ontario School Boards' Co-operative Services Program Annual Report. (1997)

45   Letter to Attention of Don Shanks, Solicitor from R.F. Robinson, Senior Counsel Ontario Ministry of Education. (November 28, 1997)

46   The Northwestern Ontario School Boards' Co-operative Services Program Resolution 7338-5 re Letter of Agreement. (December 4, 1997)

47   Memorandum to Secretaries and Principals of School Authorities purchasing Full Education Services form the Co-operative Services Program from Fred Porter. (May 8, 1998)

48   December Conference Agenda sponsored by The Northwestern Ontario School Boards' Co-operative Services Program and OISE/UT Northwestern Centre. (December 2, 3, 4, 1998)

49   Memorandum to Secretary-Treasurers from Fred Porter regarding Restructuring Funds. (September 4, 1998)

50   Northwestern Ontario School Authorities and The Northwestern Ontario School Boards' Co-operative Services Program "Proposed Membership and Services Fee Model". (April 8, 1999)

51   Article form The Chronicle Journal (October 5, 1999) and Article from the Thunder Bay Post (October 8, 1999).

52   Expert from the Minutes of The Board of Directors Meeting. (April 27, 2000).

53   Ontario Regulation 280/00 made under the Education Act. (May 11, 2000)

54   Northern School Resource Alliance Board of Directors Teleconference Minutes. (June 7, 2000)

55   Excerpt from Northern School Resource Alliance Board of Directors. (July 21, 2003)

56   Letter from Gerard Kennedy, Minister of Education to Shelley Martel, MPP Nickel Belt. (January 27, 2006)

57   Minutes Northern School Resource Alliance Board of Directors. (September 8, 2006)

58 Excerpt from Northern School Resource Alliance Board of Directors. (October 11, 2006)

59 FOI Contentious Issues Briefing Note Ontario Ministry of Education. (February 20, 2007)

60 Letter to Michael A. Brown from Kathleen Wynne, Minister of Education (April 3, 2007) and letter to John McInnis, Chairperson and Ms. Devona Crowe, Supervisory Officer for Atikokan RCSS Board from Bill Mauro, MPP (April 17, 2008).

61 Excertp from Northern School Resource Alliance Board of Dreictors. (May 6, 2008)

62 Letter to Fred Porter, Supervisory Officer from Ben Levin, Deputy Minister of Education (June 1, 2009) and Letter to Diane Laybourne, Chairperson from Kathleen Wynne, Minister of Education (June 1, 2009).

63 Isolate Board and District School Board Amalgamations as of September 1, 2009.

64 Article from The Chronicle Journal "School Amalgamation Without Consultation". (June 20, 2009)

65 Letter to Kathleen Wynne, Minister of Education from Armand Giguere, Chairperson. (August 2, 2009)

66 Letter to Armand Giguere, Chairperson and Terry Swanson, Vice Chairperson from Kathleen Wynne, Minister of Education. (August 14, 2009)

67 Letter to Ombudsman Ontario from Armand Giguere, Chairperson. (August 17, 2009)

Index

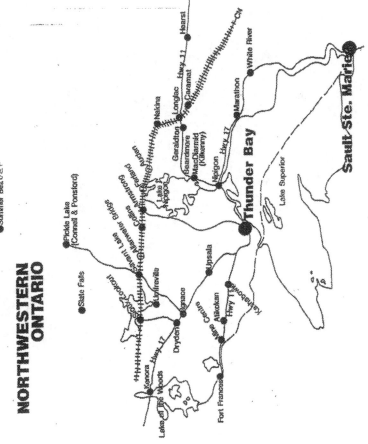

NORTHWESTERN ONTARIO

Summer Beaver

Pickle Lake (Cornell & Ponsford)

State Falls

Kenora
Lake of The Woods
Hwy 17
Dryden
Ignace
Fort Frances
Lac Seule
Atikokan
Hwy 11
Kashabowie

Savant Lake
Lac des Mille Lacs
Upsala

Sioux Lookout
Silver Water Bridge
Collins
Armstrong
Lake Nipigon

Thunder Bay
Lake Superior

Nakina
Geraldton
Longlac
Hwy 11
Caramat
Hearst
Beardmore
MacDiarmid (Kilkenny)
Nipigon
Hwy 17
Marathon
White River
CN

Sault Ste. Marie